RE-ARRANGING
YOUR
MENTAL
FURNITURE

CHANGING YOUR
FUTURE
FOR THE
BETTER

RE-ARRANGING YOUR MENTAL FURNITURE

BY

KEN GAUB

If you would like to write the author
or
schedule him to speak,
he can be contacted through:

Ken Gaub
World Wide Ministries
Y.O.U. Productions
PO Box 1
Yakima, WA 98907
U.S.A.

Phone - (509) 575-1965
Fax - (509) 575-4732

E-mail - KenGaub@aol.com
Visit out website -
http://users.penn.com/faithinaction/fian.htm

ISBN 1-57502-480-2

Library of Congress Catalog Card Number: 97-93434

Note: This book contains quotes by a number of people.
        Many of these quotes are in common use. The use
        of a quote in this book does not indicate a blanket
        endorsement by the author of all their views and
        their lives.

All scripture references are from the King James Version unless
otherwise noted.

Cover Photo by Terry M. Wowchuk - Finelight
Winnipeg, Manitoba, CANADA

Cover Artwork by Robert D. Payne
Payne Co. Design Group - Yakima, WA

Printed in the U.S.A. by

Morris Publishing
Kearney, NE 68847

ENDORSEMENTS

Ken Gaub is one of the most inspiring persons I know. His ministry is always impactive, and he is ever on the alert to personally lead people to Christ. Many lives are always touched for God. The last time he was at Cypress Cathedral, I had our marquee along the highway read:
KEN GAUB
INSPIRATIONAL
MOTIVATIONAL
INDESCRIBABLE

Rev Dwight Edwards
Cypress Cathedral
Winter Haven, FL

God has given Ken Gaub the ability to present powerful truths and principles with humor and a motivational punch. I've wondered what his vantage point is that enables him to see things so uniquely that when you look through Ken's eyes, you feel as if you're seeing them for the first time.

Willard Thiessen
"It's a New Day"
Trinity Television, Inc.
Winnipeg, Manitoba, CANADA

Ken Gaub is a great communicator. He finds where you are, then leads you on a journey that involves laughter, instruction, inspiration and God's principles. When you hear Ken, you are motivated to be all that God intends you to be. We love him here at First Assembly.

Rev. Alton Garrison
First Assembly of God
North Little Rock, AR

Ken Gaub is a true minister. His ability to teach using the medium of humor is delightful. His walk with God has been a remarkable journey that will inspire faith in all who hear him or read his books.

Rev. Leroy Lebeck
Trinity Church
Sacramento, CA

If there is one work that describes Ken Gaub, it is *UNIQUE*. Ken is an author, gifted speaker, Bible teacher, evangelist, motivator, comedian, husband, grandfather, Christian and loyal friend. Ken is also a man on a mission with infectious enthusiasm. If you are not inspired after personal exposure to Ken Gaub, then you are also *unique*.

Rev. John Lloyd
Countryside Christian Center
Clearwater, FL

Ken Gaub is a creative soul winner, motivating others to do the same. Always behind his excitement and fun is a desire to help hurting people. He has a unique goal of keeping his scheduled appearances. He has driven all night over snowbound roads when his airline flight was canceled because of weather, and everyone else was stranded. Several hours and two hundred miles later, he was on time to speak at our church. He considered his appearance of highest priority and an emergency as an ambassador of Heaven's government.

Rev. James Menke
New Hope Christian Center
Lima, OH

Ken Gaub is known and respected all over the world. We are honored to have him and his family as members of Stone Church where I have pastored for over thirty years. He recently was our Sunday pulpit guest again. You could just feel a ripple of excitement pass through the sanctuary as he came to the pulpit. Irrefutable testimony; Ken Gaub is loved and respected at home, too.

Rev. Dale Carpenter
Stone Church
Yakima, WA

Ken Gaub is a very rare combination of preacher, motivator, author, father husband and friend. His books reflect his sensitivity in all areas of life. Ken's writing will keep you reading and growing. The humor in Ken's messages make spiritually palatable some rather heavy thoughts which would be a load to carry ,if it were not for his unique ability to give a bit of jest that does no damage to the principle, but enables it to be extremely effective.

Don Lyon, D.D.
Faith Center
Rockford, Il

DEDICATED TO:

My Parents: John and Millie Gaub, whose encouragement, daily (sometimes hourly) prayers, support and faith helped me keep on going.

My daughter Becki: Who was persuaded at the last minute to help me finish this book.

All my friends and supporters.......who believe in this ministry and continue to pray and support so we can touch the world for God. How we thank God for the harvest. The best days are just ahead.

Special thanks to pastors of the greatest churches in the world, who bring me in to minister to their congregations. I love you all.

And finally special thanks to Billy Joe Daughtery for allowing me to use "10 Commandments for Parents."

QUOTES

TABLE OF CONTENTS

FOREWORD

KEN GAUB......IS A SOULWINNER.....
Ken's heart is set on knowing God and
helping others to also know Him. He is just
as interesting in person as he is when he is
speaking to thousands. He wants people to
know Christ as savior in their lives. Ken's
ministry at Victory Christian Center in
Tulsa has always been outstanding. Not
only did the lost find Christ during his
meetings, but Christians were inspired to
win others outside the church as they went
about their daily lives.

Rev. Billy Joe Daugherty
Victory Christian Center
Tulsa, OK

INTRODUCTION

It really was never a goal, not in my wildest dreams to write books. I always thought *Authors* wrote books. Then early this morning, I asked myself the question - ***What is the main reason I am doing another book?***

IS IT BECAUSE I NOW KNOW EVERYTHING? Trust me, that certainly is not the answer.

IS IT BECAUSE I NEVER GET ANGRY OR HAVE A BAD ATTITUDE AND TREAT EVERYONE RIGHT ALL THE TIME? That isn't right either.

MAYBE AFTER ALL THESE YEARS I NOW KNOW HOW TO SUCCEED WITHOUT FAILING, SO IT'S TIME TO SHARE? That's also a long way from the truth.

MAYBE SINCE I ALWAYS PRACTICE WHAT I PREACH, I CAN TELL OTHERS HOW TO DO IT? I wish that were so. Sometimes I feel guilt when negatives hit my life. I have feelings, can be hurt, and believe it or not, I'm also human.

IT'S PROBABLY DUE TO THE FACT THAT EVERYONE LOVES ME AND I HAVE NO ENEMIES. I'm sure that I have my share. It's impossible to please everyone all the time.

MY FRIEND.......The *REAL REASON* behind authoring another book is two-fold.

1. God wanted you to hear it.
2. I love helping others find answers to life's problems.

As I was in the process of writing, I remembered many letters that I have received from all over the world about other books I have written, or because someone had seen me in person in their area or heard a tape or seen a video.

This book may not be perfect in every way. Some have read my books to look for mistakes or contradictions. I am simply teaching what has helped me. My soul burned as I wrote the following pages. Many struggle to get through a day; on the job, in their marriage or in many other ways.

I'm committed to a lifetime of helping people who need some answers in their lives. I may step on your toes, but I trust I won't mess up the shine. As you read, you will understand why I think like I do, and I trust you take steps to turn things around. You can, with God's help, because *All things are possible!*

One of the greatest positive thinkers of all time was a Jew. He lacked the opportunities that some have. He was looked down upon because he was poor. He came from the wrong area of the country. He was a simple laborer. He had to work, and still had little of this world's goods. He was never outside the boundaries of his own country. He was not "well connected." He couldn't be a "name dropper." His companions were the sick, the needy, the working class, and even crooked politicians and tax collectors. But His name was Jesus and He was the Son of God. He completely changed the world. He succeeded in His mission, when He died for the sins of the world. He can set us free.

My prayer is that:
You will find God's perfect will for your life.
You will change your attitude for the better.
You will face all challenges with a determined faith in God;
You will learn to take the opportunities that God places before you.
You will make stepping stones from our failures.
You will have a wonderful home and family.
You will make decisions that really count.

You will have health and healing.
You will be blessed financially.
You will have a honeymoon marriage. (If you are married.)
You will believe in the *Jesus Factor*.

Now....Let's get your hopes up for a great future. You can have that unbeatable thinking. You can have a correct image of who God really is and what He wants to do for you. Your tomorrows will be better than your yesterdays......is my prayer.

KEN GAUB

There are 2 sure things in life:
1. There is a God!
2. You are not Him! (and neither am I!)

1

HOW WE THINK
AND WHY

IN THIS CHAPTER:

    TOMMY BARNETT

    GEORGE BERNARD SHAW

    CHARLES F. KETTERING

    NORMAN VINCENT PEALE

    DAN WOLD

    BILLY SUNDAY

    JIM AGARD

    DAVE HESS

    ROBERT SCHULLER

    SAM SMUCKER

CHAPTER ONE
HOW WE THINK AND WHY

When the full force of "thinking right" hit me, it went deep into my heart. I began to know that I didn't think right about a lot of things, and became determined to change. You can do the same thing.

In this book we're going to deal with a lot of things concerning our thinking. Wrong thinking does not produce right results. Negative thinking will never produce positive results.

We form good or bad thoughts in our minds because of many things; our past experiences, our knowledge of God's Word, how we feel about ourselves, our general physical and emotional health and even our dreams and goals all effect our thinking.

I'm against *New Age* teaching, which is a conglomeration of many things. The *New Age* movement is not an organized, consistantly cohesive set of teachings. It borrows from many different and diverse religions and philosophies. Some solid Christian teachings are twisted and pushed out of balance and incorporated within the *New Age* umbrella.

However; there are many positive ministers to whom we could well listen, in order to change our thinking, and our future. The message of Jesus was a positive one. He taught action, not passiveness. He is our ultimate example.

We're going to talk about rearranging our mental furniture, shifting our thought patterns. It's true that we need to change how we think about situations. The Bible tells us in Proverbs 23:7 "as a man thinketh in his heart, so is he."

Yes, I know there is more to it than just thinking. Unless we act upon our thoughts, they just remain thoughts. We can change negative thinking to positive thinking. When we begin to think differently, we function differently, our future will change.

WHAT YOUR THOUGHTS DO

Your thinking can help make you a success or a failure. Your thoughts can make you a free person, or put you in prison. They can help you, they can hurt you. They can lift you, they can tear you down. They can make you love or hate, they can make you laugh or cry. They can make you advance or retreat. They can make you a winner or a whiner. Your thoughts control the way you react to situations.

Your thinking will help you succeed or cause you to struggle. Your life can grow or shrink. You can thrive or you can fail. It depends on how you think about it.

If you want God to give you miracles, you have to prepare to receive those miracles. Close the doors of your thought life to fear, envy, anger, bad attitudes. Open the doors of your thought life to miracles, answers, faith in God, the Holy Spirit, possibilities. God can help you think about the good things He is going to do for you.

You can overcome frustrations that are discouraging, and seemingly impossible situations and be defeated or you can walk tall, and whistle and laugh rather than whimper and whine.

I've often wondered why some people succeed, when they are less talented than others. They have learned to overcome, to look at situations in a totally different manner. They've faced unbelievable tragedy with faith in a God that will see them through. They are enthusiastic, they are optimistic. They have confidence. They have faith. They break records, and they make things work.

Thank God for this kind of people. I believe the greatest miracles have yet to be accomplished. I believe that the greatest churches in the world have yet to be built. I have heard ministers say that they could never build a great church like Tommy Barnett with thousands attending. Why not? Tommy is a friend, and his church touches the world and will continue to grow, but his life should be a challenge for others to do more.

The greatest moments in our lives lie just ahead. I look for it, and I think about it. I get excited about it. I'm going to receive it.

When I wake up in the morning, I think about what a great day this will be. I pray and tell the Lord of my love for Him, that I'm going to serve Him and obey Him. I say, "God whatever you're doing today. I want to be a part of it. I'm not asking you to only bless what I do. Please let me do what you are blessing. Fill my thoughts and my mind with good positive things for today. I may face many challenges, but I know you'll see me through."

Every morning a wonderful thing happens to me. It makes no difference where I am in the world. It happens every day. I wake up breathing. That's exciting. Think about it.

You should get up in the morning praising God for another day. Refuse to let yesterday or past problems enter your mind. "Submit yourselves therefore to God. Resist the devil, and he will flee from you," James 4:7. Take your stand at the beginning of the day.

It's important how we think. Our mind is a billion dollar gift from God. No computer can match the capabilities of our mind. We seldom tap even a small portion of its potential. Romans 8:5,6 says, "For those who live according to the flesh set their minds on the things of the flesh, but those who live according to the spirit the things of the spirit, for to be carnally minded is death, but to be spiritually minded is life and peace." God made our minds for a purpose.

Our mind cannot be physically touched or seen. It is like a computer program that is written on our brain. Just like a computer, we make decisions and draw conclusions from the material that's fed into our mind.

Unlike a computer, our minds have the unique ability to draw more than just one set of conclusions from each situation.

Few people think more than once or twice a year. I have made an international reputation by thinking once or twice a week.
George Bernard Shaw

WHO ARE WE?

How we think can even determine how we will feel. We live in a world that is so phony and full of pretense that we really need to think about who we really are. The way we carry ourselves, the way we walk, the way we talk and even the clothes we wear and how we dress all reflect the way that we actually think.

You can't have a better tomorrow if you're thinking about yesterday all the time.
Charles F. Kettering

It's amazing how many of our crises or challenges could be solved if we'd just use common sense and think things through. Many times we try to do everything else because thinking seems to be such a hard thing to do.

You may say, it's my job, it's my family, it's my challenges that make me the way I am. The real truth of the matter is the way you think about those things and react to them makes you what you actually are.

Success doesn't just fall out of the sky onto your head. You do things that set it in motion. You will never change the way things are in your life until you change the way you think. Then you will change the way you do things.

You might say, Ken, why is my thinking so important? One reason is that our thinking affects our total believing. Our believing controls the way we talk. It becomes a cycle. We can get caught up in the wrong cycle. Faith in God will help us break negative cycles in our lives, and tear down the strongholds of Satan, thus helping us develop the quality thinking that the Bible teaches. It's so refreshing, so exciting to think in a positive manner. So let's eliminate the negative thoughts in our lives, and replace them with positive thoughts. No wonder Paul stated, "whatsoever things are true, ... honest, ... just, ... pure, ... lovely, ...of good report; if there be any virtue, and ..... praise, think on these things." (Philippians 4:8 KJV).

> **Change your thoughts,**
> **and you change your world.**
> **Norman Vincent Peale**

When negative thoughts hit you, interrupt those negative thoughts and recall the good things that God is blessing you with. Think about the good things. When a challenge hits your life, start thinking differently about that challenge. Start looking *for* the answer, instead of *at* the problem. Look for as many possible solutions as you can. Refuse to let the problem wear your spirit down.

When bad situations come our way, many people take a negative approach. They look for the things that won't work instead of the things that could work.

When you think correctly, it can help you overcome all of life's limitations. It will change your world. It will help you jump over every obstacle. I firmly believe that your life will move in the direction of your most dominant thoughts. I think about winning people to Christ, so my life moves in that direction.

> **The negative thoughts that hit our lives are the worst bandits that we'll ever face.**
> **Dan Wold**

We make two errors. We overestimate the other fellow's brain power and underestimate our own. Because of that, we fail to do things. Someone comes along who doesn't worry about brain power, and he is able to have miracles happen.

> **More men fail through lack of purpose than through lack of talent.**
> **Billy Sunday**

Many things begin in our thought life. A person who watches pornography will end up thinking that it is normal. Rape, sexual violence, divorce, murder, robbery all begin with thinking.

Isaiah 26:3 says, "You will keep him in perfect peace, whose mind is stayed on you, because he trusts in you." We all think about things other than God, we think about our families, food, sleeping, traveling. Our mind needs to be focused upon God. People think about romance, about material things, some think about drugs and pornography, others think about New Age, etc. They don't think about the things of God. Some people don't even know what they're thinking.

When you start giving up because of financial obligations and being in debt, interrupt those thoughts with the promises of God. His desire is to prosper your life in a special way.

II Corinthians 10:4,5 state "For the weapons of our warfare are not carnal, but mighty in God, for pulling down strongholds, casting down arguments, and every high thing that exhalts itself against the knowledge of God, bringing every thought into captivity to the obedience of Christ." Paul says that the greatest warfare is in our thought life. We need victory over negative thoughts that control our life.

Nothing in life changes unless we choose to change a certain thing. Most of us don't have to do anything special to become overweight. It takes effort to lose the extra pounds and keep them off. It doesn't take much effort to have a messy house, but it takes discipline to keep it neat. Our mind is the same way.

It can become messy, because Satan and the negative world around us will produce all kinds of things that will cause it to be messed up. It takes work to keep it clean and keep our thoughts positive.

"It is the thought life that pollutes." (Mark 7:20 LB) Our thoughts can be deadly to us.

We all think or meditate every day. Meditation is merely thinking about something for a long period of time. When you control your mind, you control your thinking. In Colossians 3:1-5, 9 and 10, we are told to set our minds on things above, not on the things of this earth. Set your thought life on the things of God. In Isaiah 55:7-9, God says that His thoughts are not our thoughts. We need to forsake our own thoughts and begin thinking like God wants us to think.

We must start thinking that we are going to be better parents. We need to be thinking about having better relationships with those around us. We need to be thinking about prospering financially. We need to focus on keeping the things around us orderly and neat. We can become an excellent person, and start thinking the way God wants us to.

WORLDLY THINKING

It's amazing how our country thinks. In today's world, we want instant solutions. We don't think things through as we look for quick answers. There are one hour photo labs, one hour dry cleaners, drive through windows, fast delivery for pizza. We want things to be instant, even relationships, finances, weight loss. We live in a microwave world. We want it done NOW.

Wrong habits, lustful ideas, envy, anger, strife, jealousies can only bring harm to your mind. Your mind can become the devil's playground. It is the entrance to your soul. If Satan can get your mind, he's got your soul.

Satan is out to destroy us. Television conveys the impression that immorality and homosexuality are normal. The forces of the world do not condemn adultery and fornication. Some people say - -

1. Why get married, we'll just live together. Others are doing it, it's okay.

2. Why have proper diet and exercise, that's too much work.

3. I don't know how to fix my finances. More credit must be the answer.

4. Children are such a pain, I'll have an abortion.

5. We don't need a relationship, we need sex now.

6. I don't need a job, if I could pull a few strings, I can live off the government.

7. Why clean the house, it'll just get messed up again. Why wash the car, it's going to rain.

That's what's gotten America into our present situation. We need a shift in our thinking.

We have gone so far in our loss of values. That's why in America, everyday several thousand unwed girls between 15 and 19 have babies. That's why kids take guns to school. That's why over 50 million Americans are hooked on nicotine. That's why over 15 million are alcoholics. That's why over 3 million are on cocaine and over 2 million on IV drugs.

USE YOUR HEAD FOR SOMETHING
BESIDES A HAT RACK.
Jim Agard

Write down your problems, then start thinking about them in a different manner. Shift your mental gears.

If you plant an acorn in the ground, an oak tree will grow. If you plant peas, you will harvest peas. If you plant strawberries, you will get strawberries. As we sow, we reap. The same is true of our thinking. Bad actions come from bad thoughts. Good thoughts produce good actions which produce good results. It requires thinking right.

Sometimes we need to not "worry" too far in the future. (Don't get this confused with setting long term goals.) Jesus prayed, "Give us this day our daily bread." Learn how to live daily with your thought life. Think, today will be a great day. All fears and worries will be gone. God will see me through. I'm not going to worry about next year, today I just want to take care of today. I know God will help me. Your thoughts will produce the energy that you need. God wants you to start believing his word and thinking that all things are possible with God. Read Mark 9:22,23.

Believe that God has miracles in the making for you. Start thinking in the way of believing. Quit thinking about the past, about the hurts, about those who have cheated you. Start living by faith and start thinking about what God can do. It will set your soul afire. It will do great things for you.

Quit being afraid of how others think and begin wondering how God thinks. Have the possibility of miracles.

SMALL AND BIG THINKERS

The way we think is more important than the intelligence we possess. Small thinkers say things differently than big thinkers. When you think you can do something great, you usually do. When you don't think you can do it, you usually don't, because you start thinking and saying that it's going to be a long, hard process, and it goes that way.

Thinking big and believing God for big things is important in our lives. To be a successful thinker does not require a super intellect. The size of our thinking determines the size of our accomplishments. We need to enlarge our thinking. Think a little bigger, think a little greater. Think a little higher, a little nicer.

If you say something won't work, and set about to prove that it won't work, you are thinking small. But if you say it will work and set out to prove that it will, you have hope of something greater.

People say, "count me out, it won't happen." Say instead, "count me in, it will happen." If you say that there's no use trying, you've already failed. Instead just keep trying until you find a new way to make this thing work. It's how you think about it.

You sometimes have to look at what could be instead of what is right now. Ephesians 3:20 says "The Lord is able to do more than we can ask or think." I can think pretty big, but God is greater than my abilities to even imagine.

We can choose to use our thinking in a positive way or to doubt and go on as we are.

> **Your emotions and actions are the belated announcement of what you have been thinking.**
> **Dave Hess**

You can't think poverty and have wealth. You can't think sickness and have health. You can't think failure and have success. Don't limit your thinking.

Human behavior is amazing and puzzling. People who command the most respect are the most successful. Thinking helps make that happen. We receive the kind of treatment we think we deserve. If you think you are inferior and worthless, you may be making a self-fulfilling prophecy. If you think you are unimportant, you're probably right. If you think you are important and can achieve and you are a special creation of God, a unique personality, you are.

To gain respect, you have to believe you deserve it. Look important, act important, talk important, not arrogant. We need first class thinking. Small thinking people will hold you back from reaching goals. It's been said that we if we help make others successful, we will also become successful.

Success can depend on the support of others. Our thinking about other people must be right.

Set your standards higher. Think that you will succeed and improve everything in your life. We've all heard it said, "If every member were a member like me, what kind of church would this church be." Do you think positively about yourself? your family? your job or your business? We need to put these principles to work.

Take time to think about things, think success, believe for success, have faith for success. Believe God will give you the success that He desires to give you.

Think differently about how to handle things. Have a shift in thought patterns. Rearrange your mental furniture.

No person would go into the world half dressed; wise people consider themselves well dressed when their mind is wearing a positive idea as a shield against negative forces in the world.

Dr. Robert Schuller

Paul stated in Philippians 4:13 that we "can do all things through Christ which strengtheneth" us. Sometimes we talk ourselves into being a total failure by talking negatively. We say aloud, "I can't make it, it's impossible, I'm fed up." Our thinking is moving in the wrong direction. We need to tell ourselves, "I can do all things. Things are going to change, with the Lord's help. The possibilities are tremendous.. I'm looking for answers. I'm a problem solver. I believe God will see me through."

Start saying every day:

Jesus is in my life. (Be sure that He is.)
God has made me a unique creation.
I'm looking forward to a great future.
Days of opportunity are here now.
Great things will happen.
I'm going to stay cheerful, even when I'm not happy.
I will control circumstances.
I will interrupt all negative thoughts.
I will be a giver.
I will obey God.
All my problems are simply opportunities.
I can do more than I think I can.
I'm enthusiastic about the future.
I have God given energy.
I am a winner, not a whiner.

I will use challenges as stepping stones.
God will help me to tap the necessary
resources to succeed.

I'm sure we've all seen how positive thinking people have reached goals, and turned their dreams into reality. They've taken the problems that they faced and turned them into victories. Their lives have been transformed. Jesus said that if we have faith as a grain of mustard seed, we can say to this mountain be removed and it will move. Nothing will be impossible to us. Let's have a shift in thinking and change to the way God wants us to think.

You need to take thirty minutes
a day with paper and pen and Bible
and just think.
It can change your life.

Sam Smucker

NOTES

Shift your thinking:

1. What areas of my thought life are based on the Word of God?

2. What areas of my thought life are carnally based?

3. What things do I think about that have produced negatives in my life?

4. What things do I think about that have produced positives in my life?

5. What things do I think about that hinder my future?

TOP THREE CHANGES TO MAKE!

1.

2.

3.

2

GOD'S WILL

IN THIS CHAPTER:

CHAPTER TWO
GOD'S WILL

God has a blueprint for your life, and for mine. He has a plan. His carefully laid out plan for salvation is part of His plan for each one of us. It is not His will that anyone misses heaven. It doesn't matter what has happened to us or where we are in our life, God has a plan for us. Your failure or success depends on letting God work out His plan, His will in your life.

> **Sometimes God doesn't tell us His plan because we wouldn't believe it, anyway.**
> **Carlton Pearson**

I don't believe that anything happens by chance with God. It is God's will that you are reading this book right now.

Do you know the direction that God has for your life? Do you know the plan that God has for you? Is the plan laid out? Do you understand it? Do you understand why you need a plan? Have you talked to God about it?

GOOD THINGS

It is God's will that good things happen to you. Because God has a perfect plan for your life, it's His will that certain things happen.

Romans 8:28 states that "all things work together for good to them that love God." It does not say that everything is good, but that God can take everything, good or bad, that crosses our pathway and cause it to work to our advantage. Does God allow suffering in the life of a Christian? Does He even arrange it? Read on.

God will take the broken, messed up pieces of a ruined, wasted life and use them to build a life that brings honor to His name. That is the ultimate in recycling.

Have you ever made the decision to go for God's perfect will, not just His permissive will? God will often permit us to have our own way, even when

He has a better way, if we insist. Unlike many of us, God is a gentleman who will not impose His will upon us, even when He knows that we are wrong.

How do you know that you have made the right decisions about His will? Sometimes people chase things that turn out to be harmful to them, because they don't go by Biblical guidelines.

Start by searching the Bible, God's written Word. Certain things are specifically either commanded or forbidden. Other things are implied by principle. Seek godly advice. Write down all the pro's and con's and study them prayerfully. Use your own mind, and put all these into your own God given "personal computer." But always remember that the urging of the Spirit will never contradict what's in the Bible.

Christians are not just the hunted, but the hunter; not the attacked, but the attackers. We are God's storm troopers.
Reinhard Bonnke

It's important that we know the difference between God's will and our will. Some things are God's will, some are our will. Our will should be surrendered to Him, so that His will becomes our will.

One of the "big questions" of all time is "Why do the godly suffer? Is this God's Will?" The Apostle Peter discusses this in I Peter 1:6-7. His conclusion is "that the trial of (our) faith,.......might be found unto praise and honor."

He goes on to tell us in chapter 2, verse 21, that left us an example by His suffering, and in chapter 5, verse 10, asks God that we be made perfect, established, strengthened and settled.

Paul wrote that our "suffering produces perserverance; perserverance, character; and character, hope. (Romans 5:3-4NIV)

GOD'S WILL FOR JESUS

Even Jesus had a moment, in the Garden of Gethsemane, when He had to surrender His will to that of the Father. He knew that Father's will for Him was to take the sins of the world to the cross, and to be a sacrifice for our redemption. But as He also looked at it from the human standpoint; the pain, the agony, the suffering, the rejection, the momentary separation from the Father made the prospect so painful that He actually sweat great drops of blood.

GOD'S WILL FOR YOU

You might feel similarly at times, torn between two decisions. In your spirit, you know what to do, but sometimes you make the wrong decision, and choose something that is not God's will because the decision seems so painful. If we're going to fulfill the will of God, we have to walk in the Spirit, so we don't fulfill the lusts of the flesh. (Galatians 5:16)

Some people have given up prospective mates who didn't fit into what they knew was God's will for their lives. A friend who had not married by the time she was 26 said, "I'm sure that it's God's will for me to be married, but there's nobody in sight!" I told her not to panic, God had a living, breathing man in existence for her.

She responded in humor, "Let him breathe on me." It was only a short time until she began dating a young man whom she married a few months later. They now have two beautiful children. The marriage has been very blessed. She refused to settle for a counterfeit of God's will for her life.

People can lose their business, home and everything they possess because of their own will. It's important that our will is surrendered to Christ. It is the will of God, not our will that is important. Jesus was our great example.

Is it God's will to be sick? I don't believe that it is. He said he "wished above all things that we would prosper and be in health." It is God's will that we are blessed. Because we live in a sick and sinful world, negative things can come into our lives, sometimes because of stupid things that we have done that were our will, not His.

I believe that it is God's will to be healthy. It is a benefit that God has promised to us. A truly Christian lifestyle is a basically healthy lifestyle. We are admonished by Paul to treat our bodies with the same respect that we would treat the Temple of God. (1 Corinthians 3:16)

But if you are sick, get your eyes off of the sickness and start believing that God will turn things around for you. God wants us well. Jesus was so concerned about sickness that He took the stripes for our healing. (Isaiah 53:6) God promised that He is the Lord who heals. He promised to take sickness from the midst of us. (Exodus 23:25) Healing is of God. He sent His word and healed them.

God doesn't want to keep his blessing from you. If you are not on the receiving end of blessings, stop blaming the devil, your spouse, your relatives and friends, your circumstances. The real problem may be your own attitude about Gods will for you.

What is the will of God in your life? We need to keep the desire for that uppermost in our thinking. It is God's will for you to be blessed in every way. You can expect it.

**You are today getting ready for
a great future in the will of God.**
Rick Thomas

NOTES

1. Trust God's will for your life.

2. Believe God wants good things to happen to you.

TOP THREE CHANGES TO MAKE!

1.

2.

3.

3

ATTITUDE FOR SUCCESS

IN THIS CHAPTER:

CHAPTER THREE
ATTITUDE

Your attitude is a very important thing in your life. Life is ten percent of what actually happens to you, and ninety percent is how you react to what happens. In our lives we acquire some good and some bad attitudes.

The last of human freedom is to choose one's attitude in any given set of circumstances.
Victor Frankl

Victor Frankl, a survivor of the Holocaust, developed this philosophy during his imprisonment in a Nazi concentration camp. He chose a positive reaction to his situation rather than justifying an attitude of despair.

Faith and a good attitude are inseparable. Where one is found, the other will almost always be found also. Faith is a God given power locked inside you. The Bible states that "to every man is dealt a measure of faith." Your attitude is the key that unlocks it. If your attitude is right it will help you to create a balance to your faith.

That is very important in this day when some are off balance. I say these three things about God: 1)He is sensible, 2)He is practical, 3)He is well balanced.

There have been many times in my life when I realized that my attitude was not what God wanted it to be. Sometimes during a crisis, a person's attitude really gets lousy. Our attitude is an important ingredient in our lives and future. Only I can control my attitude, with God's help.

We need to choose to be positive and react right no matter what happens. We all have the ability to have a good attitude. We are not responsible for the attitudes of those around us, but we are responsible for our own attitude. Those who have a good attitude will usually react differently to problems of any kind than those who don't.

Sometimes we allow things from our past to mess up our present attitude. When we do this, we are giving up the control that God has granted us.

No one has ever given me a bad attitude. I do that on my own, by allowing what someone else says or does to affect my feelings and my actions. God has given us the power to have a great attitude. God gave us control over our minds, which affects our attitude. Most people that I know who have great dreams and high goals also work on having a good attitude.

Your attitude speaks to others. It can say, I love you, I think you're important, I'm jealous of you, I didn't like what you did, I'm tired of my job, I don't like this thing. You speak without a sound. Attitudes are mirrors of what we are thinking, and show up in spite of what we say.

You can know how someone likes his job by his attitude. You can often detect attitude by the tone of a person's voice. It can be seen through his enthusiasm, or by a handshake. A person's eyes can reveal much of his attitude; whether or not he meets your gaze directly. The sincerity of a smile also reflects attitude.

Handwriting can also show attitude. The manner in which you walk and talk and dress also indicate attitude.

Some of us need to practice having a good attitude. I often have to work on my own attitude. I don't have much patience with the way others do things if I feel they are inept or inefficient.

> **The greatest revelation of our generation is the discovery that human beings, by changing the inner attitudes of their minds, can change the outer aspects of their lives.**
> **William James**

Some people have a mental malignancy. Their attitude predicts trouble. It predicts obstacles. It predicts fear, doubt and pessimism. It is an attitude of worry. It shows a lack of confidence. It sees failure. They permit it in their lives.

> **Never complain about what you permit.**
> **Mike Murdock**

Sometimes our "pet peeves" mess up our attitude. We can keep a good attitude and be free from aggravation, if we want to. The decision is ours.

Being judgmental can cause us to be disgusted at others because they don't perform up to our standards of behavior. We need an attitude of understanding for others. We need a shift in the way we think about others and the way they do things.

A SHIFT IN ATTITUDE

Listen to this story. It illustrates a shift in attitude:

You just purchased a brand new car. You don't want to even leave footprints on the mat. As you drive carefully down the road, You see a small boy waving frantically. As you pass him, he throws something at the car. You hear a noise as a rock hits your fender, and realize that he has possibly dented the door.

You slam on the brakes, back up, jump out and start towards the child, who is now running toward the house. You follow, determined to report the incident to his parents. They are going to pay for the damage!

Your blood pressure is near boiling, your attitude is vindictive. As you catch him and grab his arm, you see tears and fright. He looks up and says, "I'm sorry I hit your car, but my little brother has fallen down the stairs. He's really hurt and I needed someone to help me."

What happens to your anger, and your high blood pressure? It disappears. Why? Understanding the situation brought a shift in attitude. Your attitude has completely changed.

When you understand a situation, it will help your attitude. You often have to listen and observe those around you to truly understand.

The waitress was getting impatient as the little boy tried to decide what he wanted. It was the middle of the lunch rush, and she felt under a lot of pressure. "How much is a milk shake?" he asked.

"A dollar and a half," she answered.

"How about a sundae?"

"The same price."

"What about just a dish of ice cream?"

"That's only a dollar twenty five," was her answer.

"I'll take the ice cream."

She served it quite unceremoniously. When she returned to clear his place, she discovered a quarter placed neatly under the dish. He had the money for the more expensive items; but was unwilling to treat himself to what he really wanted, because then he wouldn't have had anything to leave as a tip.

One good way to improve your attitude is to have your confidence increased. You were born with confidence. You are confident that you will be paid for your work. You believe that your body will heal a cut. You believe that an umbrella will keep the rain from falling on your head. God's Word is a great confidence builder.

To have a good attitude, we need to learn to control negative expectations. Expectations control our life. Most people seem to believe in negative results. They say that 90% of adults think negatively, thus causing a bad attitude.

I have a friend, now in her eighties, who has spent much of her life preparing for the worst things to happen in any given situation. She was often almost disappointed when it turned out to be better than she expected.

Since our attitudes are reflected in our lives and expectations, we often receive the negatives that we expect. Job 3:25 says, "The thing which I greatly feared is come upon me." He expected tragedy.

If all sales people would have positive attitudes, expecting to sell, their sales would increase. If you ask people to describe their job: their answers usually are, I work for J.C.Penney, I work for a fertilizer company, I'm in the insurance business, I'm in real estate. Very few will respond, I sell clothing, I sell apples, or whatever. Their response is not totally positive. They don't say, I expect to make a sale in real estate. Their attitude of expectation is wrong. God wants us to have an attitude of success.

Three men are working in a rock quarry. The first man says he is breaking rocks. The second man states that he is earning his salary. But the third man says, "I'm building a cathedral." Each man is correct about what he is doing, but the attitude of the third man surely makes it more pleasant to swing the sledge hammer.

NO DRIVER

Now and again you will read that a car crashed because it had no driver. The driver had died at the wheel from a heart attack or whatever. There are a lot of people whose lives "have no driver," like the car. Someone sits in the driver's seat, even starts the engine, but they "die at the wheel" from a fatal bad attitude. Other lives end before the car is even out of the garage.

A positive attitude will always find a way to achieve the impossible. A person with a good attitude doesn't allow the negative to overwhelm him into quitting. When we change our attitudes from negative to positive, we can change our future. The difference is all in the attitude. God gives us the power to choose our attitude.

Your attitude is more important than your IQ. It's more important than your past. It's more important than the opinion of others. It's more important than your education, and any degrees you may have earned. It's even more important than either finances or present circumstances. It's more important than the people around us.

A positive attitude does not refuse to recognize the problems that may be around us. It does refuse to dwell on those problems. Some have a bad attitude because we live in a negative world, and they have allowed all the ways of a perverted world to infuse their attitude. Because of the negative world we live in, our mind can be full of garbage. We can't have a good attitude if our mind is full of garbage.

I don't like it when people dump negative things in my ear. I am not a garbage dump. However, if someone has a problem and wants help, I am there.

There are few things worse than having a bad attitude, or nicer than a good attitude. Many times our attitude becomes bad because of circumstances, what others have done, what's happened to us. Our attitude will be remembered long after those things are forgotten. Our attitude should be like what Jesus portrayed. (Philippians 2:5)

CAUSE DISCOVERED

When Clair Boothe Luce was appointed as Ambassador to Italy, she made her residence in a beautiful villa from the 17th Century. She began to notice personal physical deterioration. She was tired and began to lose weight, and had little energy. Her physical condition worsened. She sought medical aid, and discovered that she was suffering from arsenic poisoning. All her staff was checked and found to be trustworthy. Was her staff trying to poison her? Where was this arsenic coming from?

Finally the cause was discovered. The ceiling was painted with beautiful roses. The paint contained arsenic lead. A fine dust fell from the roses. Mrs. Luce was being slowly poisoned. Sometimes we're unaware of the dangers from the society that we live in. Our attitudes and concepts can be poisoned by the materialistic values of those around us. We're often unaware of it until the damage has been done.

Don't let Satan rearrange your mental furniture and do damage a little at a time until you're destroyed.

Our attitude affects others. My pastors, Dale and Mary Lou Carpenter, have positive attitudes. Thus, their son, Cal, who is also a pastor, has a good attitude. The attitudes of the staff and board at our church are positive. This in turn reflects to the congregation. None of us are perfect, so there are times when we all have to work on our attitude. Remember that your attitude affects others.

A United Airlines flight attendant asked me why I was happy and singing all the time. "Are you a Christian?" she queried. "Of course," I answered affirmatively. "I knew it," she said, "your attitude shows it."

You have an opportunity to discover God today in a way you have never discovered Him.
Peter Doseck

NOTES

1. Work on your attitude now!

2. Forget who did what to you.

3. Stop predicting problems.

TOP THREE CHANGES TO MAKE!

1.

2.

3.

4

CHALLENGES AND OBSTACLES

IN THIS CHAPTER:

> HAPPY CALDWELL
>
> SMITH WIGGLESWORTH
>
> ABIGAIL VAN BUREN
>
> WOODROW WILSON
>
> KENNETH COPELAND
>
> VAN CROUCH
>
> FANNIE HURST
>
> SIR ISAAC NEWTON
>
> NOAH WEBSTER
>
> REINHOLD NEIBUHR
>
> ST. TERESA OF AVILA
>
> DAVID LIVINGSTON

CHAPTER FOUR
CHALLENGES AND OBSTACLES

Sometimes we make big things out of nothing. A lady came up to me one day, extremely upset. Her words were, "I don't like your beard." I answered, "That's fine." "Why do you grow a beard, anyway?" she continued.

Now, I could have gotten upset and told her that it was none of her business and that I didn't like her hair. But I decided to keep sweet and turn this challenge into a stepping stone. I said, "Let me tell you what happened and one reason that I have the beard. I used to shave every day. I would cut it off, but the next morning God grew it out again. This went on for several years until I finally said to God, 'okay, God, if you want to grow it out, there it is,' and I just let Him grow it out."

She had no answer to this reasoning, and we laughed together. Every time I see her, she says, "I see God is still in control."

I tell this story as a humorous illustration that sometimes we take little things that don't really matter and make them bigger than they really are. We blow them all out of proportion and get into trouble because of it.

> **You don't go by what everything looks like. You have to go by what God's Word says, and trust God.**
>
> **Happy Caldwell**

It seems that our lives are always under construction. We keep going through the construction area. We get held up on our journey. We're always having to rebuild a road or replace a bridge or repave the surface. The construction area of our life is filled with challenges and obstacles, which sometimes even become crises, if we allow them to. At this very moment it doesn't matter how discouraged you are, you can get through it. Turn this discouraged situation into an opportunity. Jeremiah. 29:11 (NIV)says, "I know the plans I have for you, plans to prosper you and not harm you, plans to give you hope and a future."

> **Great victories come out of great battles.**
> **Smith Wigglesworth**

Those who finally succeed are the ones who use those challenges and setbacks as opportunities. They assess the situation and then move forward. They don't accept challenges as something permanent that will curse them forever. It doesn't keep them from trying again. They know failure is only temporary.

> **If you want a place in the sun, you have to put up with a few blisters.**
> **Abigail Van Buren**

Your challenges are only opportunities with a few thorns. Having an inner peace in your life comes from God. Patience also comes only from God. During a challenge, inner peace and patience are the way to insure progress through the challenge. Isaiah 26:3 says, "You will keep him in perfect peace, whose mind is stayed on you, because he trusts in you."

> **Some of us let those great dreams die,**
> **but others nourish and protect them,**
> **nurse them through bad days til they**
> **bring them to sunshine and light**
> **which comes always.**
> **Woodrow Wilson**

I used to think that it was the impatient people who really accomplished great things. I have discovered that I was wrong. Impatient people will get things started, but it's often the patient who actually see the project through to completion. They remain calm through the waiting period. They are able to ignore the turbulence. They live above it and keep a great attitude.

> **Faith opens the door to God's promise for you, and**
> **patience keeps it open until that promise is fulfilled.**
> **Kenneth Copeland**

Noah Webster spent 36 years working on his dictionary. Edison failed 10,000 times in his efforts to perfect the light bulb. Fannie Hurst received 36 rejections from the Saturday Evening Post before a story was accepted for publication. Sir Isaac Newton spent nearly 40 years before writing his "law of gravity." He stated, "What I have done is due to patient thought."

> **The battle belongs to the persistent.**
> **Refuse to let friends or circumstances defeat you.**
> **Van Crouch**

PATIENCE

Maybe you are wondering what this has to do with obstacles and challenges. I think that patience has to be involved with overcoming these things. The next time you face a tremendous challenge or a crisis in your life, try one of these two prayers.

The first one was written by Dr. Reinhold Niebuhr in 1935. It has been used many times and was adopted by Alcoholics Anonymous and distributed to American soldiers by the USO.

> *"O, God, give me the serenity to accept what cannot be changed, the courage to change what should be changed, and wisdom to distinguish one from the other."*

The second one was written over 400 years ago by Saint Teresa of Avila.

> *"Let nothing disturb thee, let nothing dismay thee, all things pass, God never changes, patience attains all that it strives for, he who has God finds he lacks nothing. God alone suffices."*

When you face a challenge, or an obstacle of some kind with another person, there are three possible solutions.

1) **The first one is to change the person.** If you try to change his thinking, it can be a very big problem. A lot of books have been written on how to change the other guy, but this can be a major problem.

2) **The second solution is to change the situation.** Avoid coming into contact with the person who is causing the problem. Some people feel that quitting the job or moving out of the neighborhood is

the answer to their problem. However, you may not be solving the problem, just taking it with you.

3) **The third solution is to change your self.** This will probably be the most satisfactory. Change your way of looking at the thing. Exhibit a desire to change. Change your attitude.

> **I will go anywhere, as long as it is upward.**
> **David Livingston**

When the 911 for emergency calling first came out we were all excited. Now we actually could get help if we needed it. God also has a 911 we can call when in need. Psalms **91:1,** says, "He that dwelleth in the secret place of the most high shall abide under the shadow of the almighty."

NOTES

1. Do not make big things out of little things. Most things are little things.

2. Live above discouragement.

3. Realize any challenge is an opportunity in the making.

4. Practice patience.

TOP THREE CHANGES TO MAKE!

1.

2.

3.

5

OPPORTUNITIES

IN THIS CHAPTER:

CHAPTER FIVE

OPPORTUNITIES

God given opportunities knock at our door. They often appear in different forms and from different directions than we expect. That is one of the tricks of opportunity. It comes in the back door disguised as defeat. It often goes unrecognized because of its disguise.

Problems are only opportunities in work clothes.
Henry J. Kaiser

Thomas Edison invented the "Edison Dictating Machine." His sales representatives had a hard time generating enthusiasm for the thing. They felt that would take too much effort to develop a market for it. This opportunity was hidden in a weird looking machine. But Mr. Barnes saw the opportunity. He was sure that he could sell it. Edison agreed to give him a chance. He sold so many of the machines that

Edison gave him a contract to distribute them. Barnes became rich. He proved that it could happen. He took the opportunity and realized the potential it had.

I believe that the biggest cause of failure is quitting before the opportunity takes hold. Don't quit just because someone tells you it can't be done. God gave us the ability to recognize good opportunities and achieve success. Success occurs when we take opportunities and failures happen when we miss them.

> **Opportunities are usually disguised as hard work, so most people don't recognize them.**
> **Ann Landers**

People don't always understand things. My parents often said things that I didn't understand. They would tell me that I "couldn't get something for nothing." Later they'd say that "the best things in life are free."

It's been said that whatever the mind can conceive can be achieved. We do need to make use of our opportunities.

> **Only he who can see the invisible
> can do the impossible.**
> **Richard Roberts**

Moses saw the invisible, chose the imperishable, and did the impossible. Don't miss out on opportunities just because they don't seem to be practical.

NOTES

1. Pray about opportunities.

2. Once the opportunity is taken don't quit when it gets tough.

TOP THREE CHANGES TO MAKE!

1.

2.

3.

6

FAILURES AND SUCCESSES

IN THIS CHAPTER:

DANNY THOMAS

ROBERT SCHULLER

ANN LANDERS

DAISY OSBORN

VAN CROUCH

BILLY GRAHAM

DEXTER YAGER

PAUL HARVEY

HENRY FORD

CHAPTER SIX
FAILURES & SUCCESSES

Let's start by defining both these terms. Success is the ability to complete the projects that one starts. Success may be defined by material possessions, but it is more than that. True success in life is measured by what a person is, not what a person has. Likewise, failure is the inability to function as a useful person.

Because such an emphasis has been placed on success in the material realm, the concept of a Christian succeeding has been given "bad press" in some circles. God is not glorified when we fail.

Some who want success don't really even know what it is. To some it is wealth, a big house, a lot of cars and to never have to work. Success seems very elusive because we measure it by what others have achieved. When we see someone in a big fancy car, we often remark as to how successful that person must be. When we hear of someone traveling the world, we feel that they must be successful in order to do that.

> **Success has nothing to do with what you gain or accomplish for yourself. It's what you do for others.**
> **Danny Thomas**

Historically, wherever the gospel is preached and practiced, the lifestyle of those who embrace it is elevated. There can be periods of persecution and hardship which temporarily interrupt this pattern, but because of the higher standard of morality and ethics, a higher standard of living is the eventually effect.

The statements that the apostle Paul made about contentment (Philippians 4:11,12; I Timothy 6:6) taken by themselves could easily be interpreted as instruction to be apathetic in all the areas of our life. I seriously doubt that Paul intended that we sit on the sidelines and make no effort to succeed. Paul must have been an extremely busy, vigorous individual, judging by what he accomplished for God.

The Bible does contain numerous admonitions against becoming obsessed with the pursuit of money to the exclusion of being concerned with spiritual values and the care of others around us. We are strongly instructed to be good stewards of whatever God entrusts to us.

Fear has a lot to do with failure. Success and God's blessing on your life and future will never jump out and attack you. People who have succeeded in anything in life have recognized causes for failure. Many great dreams have been destroyed because of a single failure. We can take failures and turn them into successes by putting God first in our lives.

Turn your scars into stars.
Robert Schuller

We have to really desire success in our lives. Many failures are due to weak wills. God gave us a will to succeed. It's nearly impossible to succeed without that will. The will to succeed will take us out of failure and use it as a stepping stone on the road to success. It will take a nervous, discontented timid person and transform him into a dynamo.

> **The Lord gave us two ends, one to sit on
> and one to think with.
> Success depends on which one we use most.**
> **Ann Landers**

You can go to the uncrowded world of success and find that most of those there have taken failures and turned them into success. They come from all backgrounds, financial strata and walks of life. They may be rich or poor, good or bad, tall or short, heavy or skinny, from all parts of the world, with different cultural and ethnic origins. They have in common that they took a failure and made it into success.

> **Absorb the principle that failure is never final, so if
> you do not succeed the first time,
> keep on trying.**
> **Daisy Osborn**

Most of those who have experienced major victories have also suffered defeats. When we succeed, we enjoy the adulation of those around us. When we really need encouragement, there are not so many to be found who are ready to offer encouragement. No one likes to be around what they consider to be a failure.

Failure can be viewed as a temporary setback. That's for those who really want to succeed. Every time you fail, you can salvage something from the failure.

Decide to do it. It doesn't matter what goes wrong, whether it's in church, in your business, on your job, at home or with your car, you can make it a stepping stone. When we succeed, we want everybody to know. But when we fail, we tend to pull back into a shell; we don't want others to know. At times like this, really true friends will come and lift you up and help to see you through. Some will call you a loser and not offer to help, because they believe you are whipped.

When you tell yourself that you're whipped, you lose the ability to conquer the problem. You will feel whipped, act whipped and stop trying. When you say that you can do it, It becomes God talking through you. You feel that you can make it, you can succeed.

Look at your setbacks and turn them into pavement on the road to the success. Assess your weaknesses and mistakes, look things all over and decide where you need to change. Begin to make those changes. Try a different route. Look at the bright side. Trust God to help you find a better way to attack the situation.

MOTIVATION

Sometimes the difference between success and failure is the motivation. Some people are happy in life, while others are always disgruntled. If we want to turn our failures around, we need a positive motivation. It will move us to make things happen.

> **Winners are ex-losers who got mad.**
> **Van Crouch**

A well motivated person has purpose, direction and energy. They have whatever it takes to make it happen. They know success is imminent. Without motivation, you will remain a failure and never find the answer. If you are motivated to succeed, failure will never hold you back. You believe that "all things are possible." (Mark 9:23) You believe that it will work. You know that failure is only temporary and are motivated to succeed.

To be truly successful, you need to believe in God. Success is not necessarily a huge thing. It is basically two things, 1) knowing what God wants you to do and 2) doing it.

When Billy Graham comes into a town, he draws the attention of the news media. He has huge crowds of people and thousands make decisions for Christ. Traffic on the freeways and side roads becomes snarled for a time. He is a success.

A missionary to Alaska travels for days by dogsled to minister in a village of less than 10 people. All of them find Christ. He is just as successful. Each has done what God asked him to do.

When we understand why we have failed, it's easier to go on to success. We need to understand certain things. When my grand kids were small, we played "make-believe monsters." I would tell stories and we'd play games. I would knock on the door or under the table and say, "Oh oh, monsters!" Their eyes would get big as we all looked around for the monster. We all knew it was a game. After a while, they discovered that Papa was the monster and there was no need to be afraid. We had a lot of fun. I wish we could deal with our adult monsters as easily as the grand kids and I did.

Real and pretend are nearly interchangeable for a small child. Many people carry monsters of failure around that keep them from succeeding. They have unfounded feelings of worthlessness and worry and fear and unforgiveness and negative emotions that rob them of their ability to reach success.

Surveys have been done which asked people what they wanted most from life, they list many things. They want 1)success, 2)health, 3)happiness and 4)recognition. Love only ranks fifth.

A lust just for money is wrong, but a desire to have resources in order to be able to give and bless others is acceptable. An attitude of failure is contagious, others can catch it from us. Parents unwittingly can pass it on to their children.

In the story of Gideon (Judges 7-8), God shows Gideon that less is sometimes more. Almost 32,000 men were sent home, and with only a band of 300, Gideon slew the mighty army of the Midianites, which numbered more than 100,000.

**Failure is not failing to meet your goal.
Real failure is failure to reach as high as you possibly can.**
Robert Schuller

Failure is a spirit from hell that will destroy you. Victory comes from heaven and will lift you up. Jeremiah 1:8 says, "Be not afraid of their faces, for I am with thee to deliver thee." He will take us from failure to success. Exodus 14:13 "Fear ye not, stand still and see the salvation of the Lord." Deuteronomy 20:1-3 "When you go out to battle.... be not afraid... for the Lord thy God is with thee."

God promised to take us through whatever the circumstances are and lead us to victory. God wants you to win when you battle against failure. No problem is greater than God's victory in your life.

Don't look at the size of the problem. It may seem much bigger than you are. Through God, you will succeed. You will be victorious. **You will be successful**, you are not under the curse of failure. You are under the blessing of God when you put Him first in your life.

> **No man will ever truly know that he has succeeded until he has experienced an apparent failure.**
> **Robert Schuller**

Some fear failure. It haunts them day and night. It fills their mind with fears. It causes them to lack the confidence that God has placed within them to be a success.

Some people will try to destroy your confidence. They want you to fail. Paul wrote, "Greater is He that is in you than he that is in the world. How can you overcome the fear of failure? Jesus said, "You shall know the truth, and the truth will set you free." (John 8:32)

Psalms 112:7,8 tells us that when we trust the Lord, we will not be afraid. We stand on the Word of

God. Jesus also said that if His words "abide in us, we shall ask what ye will, and it shall be done unto you." (John 15:7) That doesn't sound like failure, that sounds like success to me.

Let's dream big dreams and trust a big God.

A dream unrealized is a dream imprisoned by the enemy of all enemies -- the fear of failure.
Set that dream free by determining that you will make it happen.
                                                          Dexter Yager

---

You "are more than conquerors through Him that loved" you. (Romans 8:37) God has built a shield around you, failure cannot enter in there. You are going on to be a success because that is what God desires for you in every avenue of your life.

Quit looking at past failures. Disregard fears and frustrations. Start believing the word of God. Allow yourself to become rooted in victory and success in your life. God is your strength and your power. Say it aloud many times each day. "God is my strength and my power. I'm going to believe God.

Fear is not to be in me. Perfect love casts out fear. I will not let Satan invade my soul. I will stop agreeing with the devil. He has no legal right to make me a failure. God will make me a success."

If you are one of the people who say they don't believe in talking positive, then go ahead and talk negative and be a failure. God wants us to talk positive. We are victorious because He is victorious. We will have the answer because He is the answer. Our lives are successful because God made us to be successful. We were born to be successful, to overcome Satan and failure.

David said that he wouldn't be afraid. (Psalms 56:11) "In God will I put my trust, I will not be afraid what man can do unto me."

You can laugh at your failures and say, "Satan, I am making my failure a stepping stone. I will achieve and succeed like God wants me to. I've stepped on failure and fear and frustration and anxiety, and made them stepping stones." That's how we climb the ladder to the answer that God has for us. He said, "I wish above all things that you would prosper, and be in health." (II John 3)

I have strong confidence in God that He wants me to be a total success in every area of my life. I have faith in Him, I stand on His Word. I am an overcomer. It will happen.

You need to say, The failure spirit is out of my life. Failure comes when you yield to a spirit of failure. You can rejoice and be happy. You can believe that God will see you through. When failure strikes or trouble comes, you can laugh at it and thank God for future successes.

> **Failure is never final,**
> **and success is never ending.**
> **Robert Schuller**

The first impulse we have is often to believe that because we failed before, we will do so again. We need to laugh at the problem, the apparent failure. Have a wonderful time. God is fixing to bless you. You're going to cross the Red Sea and not fail the test. Worship God, refuse to allow a spirit of failure to get hold of you. Rise above those problems and failures and frustrations and begin to rejoice in the Lord.

Your apparent failure is not really your problem. Your ignorance of why the failure occurred is the real problem. When you learn to trust God, you know that He will bring victory to you, and make you a success. The circumstances don't matter because God is bigger than the circumstances. He's bigger than the negatives around you that tear at your faith. You may be fearful of failure, negative circumstances may push you, but you can rebuke the circumstances just like Jesus rebuked the wind and the sea.

For me, success is........to leave the woodpile a little higher than I found it.
Paul Harvey

Maybe you feel that the problem is a major thing in your life. God will fight our battles. We don't have to worry. We can come boldly before God and trust Him. We have a choice to yield to failure or to yield to God. I sleep well at night because I give all my problems to the Lord, He's awake all night anyway.

Abraham and Sarah were childless. They were concerned about the situation, because it was a failure. When they tried to correct the situation on their own, the birth of Ishmael was the result. The miracle that finally came from God came in spite of their efforts, not because of them. When we try to do it our own way, we often get in trouble. Abraham didn't stagger at God's promise.

Do you fear failure? Give it all to God. Let God make havoc of the enemy. When Abraham took his mind off the circumstances, off His and Sarah's age, a miracle happened. They went from failure to success. God is also your refuge. Tell yourself that daily.

I try to be so conditioned by God's word that I refuse to fail. The devil may try to sidetrack me, but I will keep my confidence in God. I believe that I will have victory. The battle is the Lord's.

The Bible is full of examples of God turning seeming defeat into victory. Stumbling doesn't mean defeat. Refusing to get up and try again is what makes for defeat.

Do you have time to succeed, or are you so busy failing that it's impossible. You will never float into success.

> **"Failure is an opportunity to begin again, this time more intelligently."**
> **Henry Ford**

NOTES

1. Start trusting God for success.

2. Take any failure and turn it into a success.

3. Stay positively motivated.

4. Reminder, success is:

> a. Knowing what God want you do to.
>
> AND
>
> b. Doing it.

TOP THREE CHANGES TO MAKE!

1.

2.

3.

7
FAMILY AND HOME

IN THIS CHAPTER:
BILLY JOE DAUGHERTY
NATHAN GAUB
DAN GAUB
REBEKAH GAUB SEGURA
JAMES DOBSON
DWIGHT EISENHOWER

CHAPTER SEVEN
FAMILY AND HOME

In I Corinthians chapter thirteen in the amplified Bible, we are told that Love never points out the faults or past failures or is critical of the others in our family. Sometimes we don't do the right thing with our family, even our children. I wish that I had time to live over the growing up of my children. I don't think I took them in my arms enough, or prayed with them like I should have. I should have reached out and touched them and showed them that I cared more than I did.

Mark 10:13-16, tells us of the love that Jesus showed to children. He admonished the disciples to be more child-like. Jesus wasn't up tight with the children, he picked them up and blessed them. We often become impatient with the immaturity of children. Their noise and mess becomes upsetting to our adult sensibilities.

I love the book "Making Your Home a Home," by Billy Joe Daugherty. He has 10 commandments for parents that will help us improve our relationship with our children. I am quoting by permission.

1. "Thou shalt start with thyself." Parents need to set an example for their children to follow. We can't tell them to do something that we are not doing ourselves. My daughter, Becki, was trying to teach the grand kids to sit down to eat, but we adults were standing and walking around the lunchroom. We can't tell them one thing and do another.

2. "Thou shalt be more concerned about relationships than rules." We all have rules. We can't totally eliminate them. Rules and guidelines are a necessity. But we have to build a relationship, and love our children as we build that relationship.

3. "Thou shalt impart the faith." We need to discuss spiritual things with our children. Age appropriate Bible reading and stories are a must. Teach them very early to pray and to love God and the things of God. Deuteronomy 6:5-9

4. "Thou shalt learn to listen." My wife was better at this than I was. Our children listen to us more readily when we take the time to also listen to them.

Listening is not easy, most of us would rather talk. Instead of listening, we are only waiting for a pause when we can add our input.

5. <u>"Thou shalt spend time with thy children."</u> That has always been hard for me. In early years, I felt that my "ministry" was more important than my family. There didn't seem to be enough time to do the things that I felt were important, and taking time from the family seemed to be the easiest way to get more time for what I felt needed to be done. God had to change some of my priorities.

We need to build relationships while they are small if we want good communication when they are grown. I often regret that I didn't take more time for fun with them when they were growing up. I know that I frequently neglected our daughter, Becki, because I felt that girls should be with their mother and boys with their father. I didn't realize how wrong this was. I was stuck in the traditional idea that boys did boy things and girls did girl things. I didn't realize until much later how much resentment was built up by my seeming favoritism for our sons, Nathan and Dan.

Now, however, Becki is a major part of the ministry. She is extremely efficient and I can always trust her to make the right decision.

6. "Thou shalt acknowledge thy faults as a parent." James 5:16 We hate to say that we're sorry, that we made a mistake. We hate to ask our children to forgive us. It just isn't in us. Aren't we in charge?

7. "Thou shalt keep a sense of humor." That's easy for me. Laughter is good like medicine, the Bible says.

8. "Thou shalt treat thy children equally." I've already told you about my error with mine. Even though you can't always treat them identically, because they are not alike, they can be treated equally.

9. "Thou shalt use discipline." That is extremely important. We don't abuse them, but there must be consequences to negative behaviors.

10. "Thou shalt know when to let go." One of the best things you can do for your children is to teach them how to get along without you. It's hard to recognize them as adults with abilities. Our son, Dan, is an intelligent young man. He has a lot of ability,

and heads up a part of our ministry called *Future Focus,* a consulting ministry for Church Growth. He has great ideas, and is constantly surprising me. I have to be careful that I don't still look at him as a child.

There are so many attacks on the home and the family today. 1 Peter 3 Peter gives us insight into family relationships. I'm praying for my family, not only my children but my siblings and parents.

> **If America is going to survive......it will be because husbands and fathers again place their families at the highest level of their system of priorities.**
> **James Dobson**

We need to accept each other for who we are, and love each other whether or not we always agree. The degree of success that each has or has not achieved should not enter into our relationships as family. We must love each other in spite of our imperfections. If we can feel accepted within our own family, it is much easier to face the challenges which the rest of the world places before us.

God intended that the family be the basic unit of society. It is within the framework of family relationships that we learn how to deal with society in general.

Family arguments and disagreements should be settled quickly in order that our feelings don't hinder our relationship with God. Confusion and strife hinder God from answering our prayers.

You do not lead by hitting people over the head, that's assault, not leadership.
Dwight D. Eisenhower

COMMUNICATION

Good communication within a family is essential. Did you ever wonder what causes quarrels within a family? They are usually over unimportant things. People get on edge. Dinner is late. Someone spoke without thinking, or someone misinterpreted what was said. Voices were raised. Accusations are made in the heat of the argument and feelings get hurt. Other members take sides.

Things are rarely settled by quarreling. Petty things get blown out of proportion. How can these conflicts be resolved? Does it really matter that the cap was left off the toothpaste? Or that someone didn't rinse out the bathtub? Or lift the seat? Or hang the towel straight?

What if a driver cuts you off? Or someone cuts in line? Does it really matter?

UNDER ATTACK

Your home and family are under attack by Satan. He knows who you are and where you live, the car you drive and also your weakest points. God also knows about you and your family. Know that you are protected by the blood of Jesus Christ. Satan will jump on you like a chicken on a June bug. However only God knows the thoughts and intent of the heart. Satan can't read your mind. Your family can be protected by God. Believe it. Act on His word.

NOTES

1. Plan to be a better parent.

2. Believe God wants to bless your home and family.

3. Work on better communication.

TOP THREE CHANGES TO MAKE!

1.

2.

3.

8

DECISIONS

IN THIS CHAPTER:

RICHARD M. DE VOS

RONALD REAGAN

"ZIG" ZIGLAR

ABRAHAM LINCOLN

CHAPTER EIGHT
DECISIONS

Your entire life rises or falls on the decisions you make. It is important that we make right decisions in our lives. One of the best decisions that we can make is found in Matthew 6:33. Jesus said, "Seek first the kingdom of God, and His righteousness." Putting God first in our life is a major decision.

You can decide to move on to success, or fall back on failure. It's all your decision. All our decisions should be based on positive values in our lives.

Making a decision can involve risk. You may have to take a stand for what you really believe. When your values are in place and your principles are in order, it's easy to make the right decision. Your future will be blessed by your correct decisions.

Even Christians make mistakes. Some make wrong decisions based upon what they "thought"

God's word meant. Some have bad attitudes because of how they have been thinking and thus they were unable to make right decisions.

> **The only thing that stands between a person and what he wants from life is often the will to try it and the faith to believe that it is possible.**
> **Richard M. De Vos**

To make an accurate decision, you must have accurate facts. Decide that you can make it happen. Decide that you will carry through.

> **When I've heard all I need to know to make a decision, I don't take a vote, I make a decision.**
> **Ronald Reagan**

THE PLAN

Before we go anywhere, we have to first decide where we are going. Then we plan the route and the mode of transportation. Will we drive or will we fly? What vehicle will get us to our destination? We get into the vehicle, after having decided that it will get us there.

We check the fuel supply. Then we start the vehicle, put it in gear, take our foot off the brake and step on the accelerator. We follow the route to our destination.

We can't drive from here to London, because of the ocean between; we have to fly. There is no possible way for our life to have meaning unless we follow the right directions. The Bible is our route book.

In order to accomplish something, we first must know what we want to accomplish. We need to know where we want to go. If you're just out for a pleasure ride with no destination in mind, don't blame anyone else if you don't make much progress. The circumstances can't take you to success if you aren't heading in the right direction.

Decide on your destination, set your goal. Decide when you want to get there. You will be surprised at how much you are able to accomplish.

When you decide what you want out of life, what your goals are, plan the route.

> **What you get by reaching your destination isn't really as important as who you become by reaching that destination.**
>
> **"Zig" Ziglar**

A big goal must often be broken into smaller goals. But you must decide. A survey was taken of 25,000 people who had experienced some kind of failure. One major cause given for the failure was lack of decision.

When we don't make decisions, we tend to procrastinate. When we have decided what we want, we usually go after it. Make the decision to be on God's side.

EAGLES, SPARROWS AND PIGEONS

The Eagle portrays the part of us that contacts God. When we think of an eagle, we think of a bird that flies so high with so little effort. The Encyclopedia Britannica tells us that since ancient times, eagles have been used as symbols of empire, courage and military prowess. The bald eagle was adopted as the emblem of the United states, probably because of the ancient use of the symbol, and also because of the bird's magnificent majesty in flight - an almost effortless majesty of the art.

Everyone who knows me knows that I love eagles. My office is filled with all kinds of them in brass, wood, glass and photos. I'm intrigued by them. I have watched them in flight until they disappeared into the distance. You rarely see an eagle do much wing flapping. It makes a few flaps of its wings until it gets into an updraft, then it relaxes and allows the wind to do the work, continuing to climb with each circle of air. It seems so effortless. God wants us to think like the eagle, to function like it and reach great altitudes of answered prayer.

I'm afraid that we too often function like sparrows, digging in the dirt, making a lot of commotion, but not getting very far. When Jesus told us to consider the sparrow, he was referring to the fact that there are a lot of them, and they are not worth very much. Sparrows are not interested in great heights. They are looking for bugs and stirring up dust.

Some people function like pigeons, hanging out in groups on a rooftop, making noise but only making a mess. They love the sound of their own voices. At the first sound of danger, they take off in organized panic, circle for a short time, then return to the roof. They are soon busy making noise again. Their actions accomplished little. We shouldn't function like sparrows or pigeons. God told us to mount up on wings as eagles. (Isaiah 40:31)

In my years of traveling, I've seen many things in many churches. Some seem to be doing all the right things, but without much results. Some minister with great sermons that cause no changes in lives. Others use psychology and humanism, but nothing happens. It's more than going through the motions. We need to soar like the eagle, letting the Holy Spirit lead us into the presence of God.

We trust....that God is on our side.
However, it is more important that
we are on God's side.
Abraham Lincoln

NOTES

1. Make decisions based on the Bible.

2. Once made follow through.

3. Ask God to forgive you of stupid decisions you made in the past.

TOP THREE CHANGES TO MAKE!

1.

2.

3.

9
HEALTH AND HEALING

IN THIS CHAPTER:
F. F. BOSWORTH

CHAPTER NINE

HEALTH AND HEALING

As we talk about health, it is said that bad health is often used as an excuse for failure to do what a person really would like to do. It should also be said that the state of our health is not an indication of our spirituality; neither is whether we are rich or poor a good barometer of our spiritual condition.

Many doctors say that everyone has something physically wrong with them. Some people use it as an excuse. People even sometimes imagine ailments and actually develop symptoms because of worrying about them.

Statistics tell us that three out of every four hospital beds are filled with someone who has an emotionally induced illness. If people would learn how to handle their emotions, these would get well sooner.

A friend of mind had an arm amputated. His attitude was that while two arms were better than one arm, one arm and a good spirit were better than two arms and a bad spirit. His spirit was complete.

I don't think that people should worry and talk and complain about their health. Just thank God that it's as good as it is. Look for improvement.

Having good health is for many of us a decision making process at least to a point. You can decide to be healthy by eating correctly and getting proper sleep and exercise. God wants our bodies to be in good health. It is easier to maintain good health than it is to cure an illness. Good health it important.

An open wound seems to heal by itself. God created us so that the necessary cells would go to that area and cause the tissues to regenerate.

When you eat, say a piece of celery, that food has no mind of it's own, but our body is so created that it takes the nutrients in that food and uses them for the things it needs.

Bad health is very negative for your life. If you want to be healthy, do the things that make you healthy, a balanced diet, exercise and enough rest.

> Some people wonder why they can't have faith for healing. They feed their bodies three hot meals a day and their spirits one cold snack a week.
> **F. F. Bosworth**

SYMPTOMS

Don't be always looking for adverse symptoms. Don't expect illness to come or to recur. Don't talk yourself into feeling down and depressed. Reject the thought that you are getting sick. Have confidence that God wants you to be healthy. Think and talk about good health. Act alive.

God made your body. He doesn't make junk. Be confident that your body will serve you well. Resist sickness and disease and germs. Use common sense and cleanliness. Some microbes are beneficial, and necessary to digestion and other body functions. Others carry disease. Frequent hand washing during an epidemic of colds and flu is only good judgment. It's not being paranoid.

To be in health and have energy, live a clean, well-balanced life, and work towards that end. Avoid unnecessary stress, which tends to weaken the immune system.

When I pray for people, I often ask God to make their body function the way He wants it to function. His word states that it His desire that we be in health. (III John 2)

Because of sin, sickness and defects have entered into the picture. God has promised to heal us when we do get sick. Those promises are our rightful legal inheritance from God through Jesus Christ.

Some people feel that perhaps God wants them to be sick, that He sends illness. Jesus took the stripes before His crucifixion in order that we might be healed. (Isaiah 53:6)

Hosea 4:6 states that "people are destroyed for lack of knowledge." They don't know that God wants to heal them. The Bible doesn't say, "I am the Lord who makes you sick!" It says, "I am the Lord who healeth thee." (Exodus 15:26) Healing is a blessing from God. God's word promises us healing. He said that healing is one of His benefits, (Psalms 103:3) "He sent His word and healed them." (Psalms 107:20)

If God had wanted people to be sick, Jesus wouldn't have gone around preaching and healing the sick when He was here on earth. To do so would have been going against His Father. He delivered people and put their lives back together. He said he would take sickness away from the midst of us.

God is a positive personality, and our faith allows Him to act on our behalf. Satan's negative personality can also be activated in our life by our fears.

John 10:10, Jesus said that He came that we might have life, and that more abundantly. It's hard to enjoy life when we are sick. It is God's will that we are well, not that we are sick.

Some might ask why we have doctors and nurses and hospitals. They are also trying to help those who are sick to get well again. I'm not against the medical profession. God often uses them as His instruments to bring about healing.

All healing comes from God. Satan doesn't heal, he only makes you sick. I believe that God wants us to be well. He doesn't want us to die before our time, like a rotten apple falling from a tree. He wants us well.

Jesus asked the man at the pool of Bethesda, "Do you want to be well?" He told him to pick up his mat and walk. He sent His word and healed people. He brought healing to families. His ministry was to heal and help. If we resist the devil, he will flee from us. Sickness and disease have to go. (James 4:7)

NOTES

1. Believe your health should be good.

2. Exercise and eat right.

3. Believe healing is yours (if sick). It's been paid for once, don't pay again.

TOP THREE CHANGES TO MAKE!

1.
2.
3.

10
FINANCES

IN THIS CHAPTER:

HYMEN G. RICKOVER

COLONEL HARLAN SANDERS

WINSTON CHURCHILL

OSWALD J. SMITH

J. C. PENNEY

PAUL HARVEY

R. G. LE TOURNEAU

JOHN D. ROCKERFELLER

HENRY FORD

ANDREW CARNEGIE

CHAPTER TEN

FINANCES

How we think about money is important. God used people in the Bible with tremendous wealth. Adam was to rule over tremendous wealth in his day. Then sin came in, and this caused man to lose the prosperity that God wanted him to have. He was evicted from the garden.

> **All of us must become better informed. It is necessary for us to learn from the mistakes of others. We are not going to live long enough to make them all ourselves.**
> **Hymen G. Rickover**

Some say "God wants me poor. Does God really want me to have money?" I believe that God is raising up a new crop of people in this time who will believe Him, who will be action oriented, have holy boldness and have purpose. They will believe God and change their world. Their thinking will change. When

I found out that God is not need oriented, but supply oriented, it changed my life.

I really believe that God will not give us more than He can trust us with. God wants to bless us. We don't have to beg Him for it. He said, "I wish above all things that thou mayest prosper, and be in health, even as thy soul prospereth." You don't have to beg God.

If you want God to bless you, you can't be a tightwad. You need to be generous with what God has blessed you with.

> **There is no reason to be the richest man in the cemetery. You can't do any business from there.**
> **Colonel Harlan Sanders**

I believe God wants us to be good stewards of the resources that He entrusts to us. I realize that money can't buy happiness in life. Poverty can't buy it either. Money is just a tool to help us meet our needs and to help us bless others. It's a gift that God has given us.

I was not educated to think and plan finances, because the general concensus was that Jesus was coming so soon that long term financial planning was not necessary. I got farther into debt than I should have because of this (and other factors.) Finally, I started thinking "debt free," not thinking of borrowing and going farther into debt. I believe God to operate on a cash basis. I think totally differently about finances than I used to.

FINANCIAL GOALS

The Bible does not say money is evil. It's the love of money that is evil. Some say money destroys people. I personally don't believe that. Money only brings out what you already are. If you are sinful with sinful ideas and get a lot of money, you will be more sinful. If you are a good person, money will bring out more of the good in you.

We need financial goals, and plans to accomplish those goals. Debt can destroy you. Interest can eat you up. I've learned to passionately hate debt. I don't want debt to enslave me, tear me apart, destroy me and ruin me. We believe in financial freedom for individuals, for families, for churches and ministries.

God isn't glorified when we are poor and broke. It isn't necessarily spiritual to be poor, sick and broke. God is a great provider of all the good things in life. He will help us to understand that His blessings are our blessings. "The blessing of the Lord brings wealth, and he adds no trouble to it." (Proverbs 10:22 NIV)

There is a curse of poverty on some people. God wants to break that curse and turn things around for blessing. God controls all the wealth of the world. He's got the whole world in His hands. He wants to bless you so that you can bless the work of God.

Matthew 25:14-29 tells the story of a rich man who left his property in the care of some servants while he took a long trip. Two of the servants invested the money and doubled it. The third was afraid, so he just hid it. When the man returned, he was extremely displeased with that servant, even though he returned the original money to him.

Gaining and keeping money, not losing it or hiding it is the key to having abundance. The amazing point of this unusual passage is that everyone who has will be given abundantly more, and those who don't have much will lose what little they have. It doesn't seem right. You must be a good steward, a good business manager with the money that God entrusts to you. You can refuse to lose and aim to gain.

Moses told the Israelites, "You may say to yourself, 'My power and the strength of my hands have produced this wealth for me.' But remember the Lord your God, for it is He who gives you the ability to produce wealth." (Deuteronomy 8:17-18 NIV) You can't get much plainer than that.

I've met Christian people who doubt that God wants them to get or keep a job. They want to be in God's will. They feel that they should just have enough to "get by." If that is true, who will finance the work of God all over the world.

Satan has stolen a lot of people's money, but God has taken the wealth of the wicked and laid it up for the righteous. If you are faithful over what God

. has given you, heaven will respond with material blessings to our lives.

> **We make a living by what we get.**
> **We make a life by what we give.**
> **Winston Churchill**

The Bible teaches us tithing and giving. The increase of money into your life depends upon you, and upon your thinking and your believing. It depends upon your obedience to God, your tithing, your giving. Your dedication to God in tithing and giving will show up in your checkbook.

> **The real measure of a man's worth is how much he**
> **would be worth if he lost all his money.**
> **Oswald J. Smith**

People say it's bad to have things, I don't want to be rich. No, it's not bad to have things, it's bad when things have you. Joseph was a man of God. He prospered in what he did; he was blessed of God. He prospered over Potiphar's house, he prospered in prison. God sent it his way. He became second ruler in Egypt. A prosperous appearance can be an advantage in witnessing to those around you. Joseph gained. God blessed him. He continued through the time of famine to gather wealth for Egypt.

It's time for you to receive God's blessings, all that God has for you. Shampoo your mind with the Word of God. God wants us to be blessed financially. Rearrange your mental furniture about money. Start giving where it can bless others.

Don't wait for specific instructions. But at the same time, don't go into debt to make things work. Creditors will only go so far. Don't sell assets in order to live. Financial disaster can arrive, and you're still waiting to hear from God. God is not only interested in our spiritual well-being, but also in our financial well-being. If you can't pay your debts on time, and keep your word to your creditors, you had better take another look at things. Proverbs 13:22 says that a good man leaves an inheritance to his grandchildren.

LIFE CHANGED

A certain man, physically and mentally shattered, walked hopelessly through the halls of an asylum. His dreams and hopes were gone, and he was nearly penniless. He owed huge debts, and knew of no way to begin to repay them. Life itself was a burden. He heard people singing, "Be not dismayed, whate'er be tide; God will take care of you."

Suddenly the truth dawned upon him. He could hear the Lord saying, "Come unto me, all ye that labor and are heavy laden, and I will give you rest." (Matthew 11:28)

This broken man felt that he could not go any farther. "God," he whispered, "will you help me?" Immediately, defeat departed from him, and he determined from that moment on that he would serve God.

Forty five years later, this same shattered, broken, defeated man, stood at an awards banquet. He was being recognized as one of the most successful business men in the history of America. He told the story.

He was so well known for his success, that it was hard for anyone to imagine that he had ever been on the brink of complete failure. He related his formula for success. "It was Jesus and the scriptures," he said, that had burst into his troubled mind so many years ago. He had re-arranged his mental furniture.

The three points of his success were 1) Come to Jesus, 2) Be yoked with him, letting Him be the boss, 3) Learn and apply his teachings. At the time of this awards banquet, J.C. Penney was 95 years old. He still worked 8 hours a day. He was happy, healthy, successful, wealthy.

The formula worked for J.C. Penney, and it will work for you today. Success can't be measured just in money or fame. We can all have success when we trust God. You may feel like you've been ripped off by the devil, but God can turn it all around for you. He can give back everything that Satan has destroyed for you. You can reclaim it. It is God's will.

Your thinking needs to change. A simple saying is, "If things don't change, they will remain the same."

Recognize that Satan is defeated. Any victory that he wins in your life is not because God wanted it to be that way. He is doing it because you are allowing it because of the way you think and live. Don't let Satan win in your life. God has never intended that he have victory over one of His children. God wants you to triumph and be victorious.

> **Be an optimist, not a pessimist.**
> **I've never seen a monument erected**
> **to a pessimist.**
> **Paul Harvey**

God doesn't do everything for you, He wants you to do something too. God doesn't just want you to die and go to heaven, He wants you to live and go to work. He wants you to live for Him, to tithe and give and have your finances blessed. God is interested in you.

Accountability is a key concept in Christian stewardship. The basic job of a steward is to handle the affairs of another. All we have in this world belongs to God. "The earth is the Lord's, and the fullness thereof."

Dependability is another aspect. If I am accountable to God, I should also be dependable. It's a response of love and gratitude to God. How much does it take to be dependable? There are minimum standards of faith and dependability. The question is how much can I give back to God, who has done so much for me. How does God judge us?

Availability is another key concept of stewardship. If we aren't available, and not willing to give ourselves to God, it isn't likely that we'll make our finances available to him either.

When we talk about Christian giving, we usually mention tithing. Tithing is not a new concept. It predates the writing of the Old Testament. Giving one tenth of our income is first mentioned in connection with Abraham and Melchezedek. This may not have been the beginning of the practice, only its first mention. The concept of tithing has been found in almost every concept of the ancient world. It was incorporated into the Old Testament Law and the principle was endorsed in the New Testament.

BLESSED

Abraham received the promise of increase in his life. First fruits, tithing is important. Abraham gave a tenth of all he had to Melchezedek, a priest of the most high God. It pleases God. The plan is that we give of the first fruits, off the top, not from what is left.

Under the Old Testament Law (Leviticus 27:30-32) the tithe was paid yearly, at harvest time to support the Levitical priesthood. It consisted of one tenth of the harvest. Tithing is only mentioned 4 times in the New Testament. We know that Jesus and his first followers were Jews who would have almost automatically followed the laws of Tithing.

What about today's Christian and tithing? We are not legalistically bound to give a tithe, we are morally bound to give from a heart and response of love. Ten percent is a good place to start. Our giving shows our sincerity and our consecration to God. It involves our stewardship. We give, not to buy salvation, but because of our love and gratitude to God for His blessings on our lives.

Everything belongs to God. Tithing is an act of worship.

Principles for Giving (II Corinthians 8: 1-15)

R. G. LeTourneau turned the profits of his business into blessing missions in other countries. When we say the names John D. Rockerfeller, Henry Ford and Andrew Carnegie, we often think of the Rockerfeller Foundation, the Ford Foundation and Carnegie Libraries. In actuality, each of these men left large sums of money that were to be given away.

Paul took an offering from the Gentile Christians for the Jewish Christians in Jerusalem who were in need. (II Corinthians. 8:9) Paul wanted this offering to be a success. He wanted to promote unity between the factions. The Jewish Christians were somewhat hesitant about taking the gospel to the Gentiles, in spite of the charge of Jesus. They stayed around home, until persecution actually forced them from Jerusalem. This offering was intended to show brotherhood between Jews and Gentiles. It showed the principle of sharing, which is basic in the nature of God.

I don't share because I have a lot or can afford it. I share because of a deep sincere desire to bless others. I don't wait until we can "afford to tithe." I also believe that ministries should be accountable to those that bless them with finances.

Tithing will not put you in a position to bargain with God. Some people think that tithing obligates God to them, and in a certain sense, that may be true. God promised to pour out a blessing on those who tithe.

People wonder why God lets them suffer when they consistantly tithe. It seems that there should be no problems at all on those who tithe. God allows almost everyone to be tested at times.

Tithing is a commandment of God, it is not an option. It will not substitute for a genuine Christian character. Tithing doesn't take the place of being committed to God.

I remember that my parents tithed. Even when they were given food by members of the congregation, at least a tenth of it would be passed on to another minister. The truth is that if we can't be trusted with the money God has blessed us with, we can't be trusted with anything.

Everything belongs to God. When we give, we know that God has a source of inexhaustible source that He wants to bless us with. God, the wealthiest being in the entire universe, is the Chairman of our business. God has wealth beyond our imagination.

Every time I think of giving, I remember that God gave His only Son, Jesus gave His life for us. The least we can do is give of our finances. Money isn't everything, and we're not working for money, we're working for God. However, we need to give from what God has blessed us with.

Whatever gets your attention gets you. If that is money, it will get you. The scripture does not say that money is evil, but the "love of money is the root of all evil."

We need to give because of our gratitude to God. People give as memorials to those who have died. Maybe instead, we should give because a loved one didn't die, because they were spared and protected. If you're a giver, you will find reasons to give. If you're a tightwad, you will find reasons not to do so.

Most churches have 100% tithers. Some give voluntarily, God takes it from the rest one way or another. It's like the little boy whose mother gave him two quarters. One was for the Sunday School offering, the other was for something that he wanted. As he walked down the street, he dropped one, and it rolled through a grate. "Well, God," he said, "I just lost your quarter."

Our attitude toward giving has to be right. Do we tithe into the church or somewhere else? As an example, if I go into McDonalds and get coffee and fries but tell the waitress that I'm not going to pay for it there, I'm going to pay for it at Wendy's, she'll think I am crazy. The same applies to our tithing. We should support the church where we're being fed.

NOTES

1. Believe God wants you to be a good steward of the money that comes to you.

2. Set financial goals.

3. Whatever situation your in now that is bad financially, believe that God can turn it around.

TOP THREE CHANGES TO MAKE!

1.

2.

3.

11

DATING, MARRIAGE & SEX

IN THIS CHAPTER:

CHARLIE SHEDD

PAULINE H. PETERS

DALE CARNEGIE

CHAPTER ELEVEN
DATING, MARRIAGE AND SEX

The first institution created by God is marriage. God knew that man would be lonely by himself, so He gave him a companion. She was not a clone, but a unique creation of her own. She had her own needs that only Adam can supply, just as only she could supply his. "Therefore a man shall leave father and mother and shall be joined to his wife, and they shall become one flesh." (Genesis 2:4)

"And the lord God said, It is not good for man to live alone, I will make a help meet for him." (Genesis 2:18) The NIV translates this a "suitable helper."

Marriage is an institution that God has blessed. A stable marriage creates a family unit that God intended to be the basis of society. God ordained marriage and family from the very beginning. The family is the first building block of society. When the family unit breaks down, all of society crumbles. We need to put Christ first in our marriage. In today's society, absolute faithfulness isn't the norm. It should be.

"And they were both naked .... and they were not ashamed." (Genesis 2:25) They shared a wonderful intimacy. They found physical fulfillment in each other. Paul wrote, "Because of immorality, let each man have his own wife and let each woman have her own husband." (I Corinthians 7:2)

Marriage takes work. It takes commitment. It really takes a miracle for God to bring two people together who will leave families and become husband and wife, and be a success at it. It's Gods plan for a husband and wife to come together and to be a strong marriage.

Marriage isn't so much finding the right person as being the right person.
Charlie Shedd

It's a strong agreement for two to be together. "Where two ...... are gathered together in my name, there am I in the midst." (Matthew 18:20) It's a strong, holy, honorable, sacred commitment.

DATING

Sometimes young people will claim that they are dating an unsaved boy or girl in order to get them saved. Instead of the Christian lifting up the other person, more often it is the unsaved who pulls the Christian down. The dating game is a poor mission field. Dates don't always end up as marriage, but marriages are usually the end result of dating. You usually marry someone whom you have dated.

The greatest temptations come to people when they are alone and out on a date, on the beach, in a parked car, at home when the parents are gone. If you don't think the devil is going to tempt you, you are mistaken. He will overwhelm your emotions and your desires for physical intimacy that God does not want outside of marriage. God doesn't want you to be deceived, he doesn't want you to be messed up. Satan has been in this a long time, and knows how to mess you up. Rearrange your mental furniture so he doesn't destroy you.

A young man in college was being teased by friends who couldn't believe that he was still a virgin. His answer was great, "Anytime I want to, I can become like you, but you can never again be like me."

God can keep you clean and pure. If you are reading this and are not married, it'll be a wonderful moment when you can say, "I totally belong to you, and only to you."

Now don't misunderstand me, God also blesses people who remain single in life. You can be blessed either way.

When you get married, you become one. You have a mind to work together, have compassion and help one another, and honor one another. "Husbands, dwell with them according to knowledge, giving honor unto the wife, as unto the weaker vessel, being heirs together to the grace of life: that your prayers be not hindered.(I Peter 3:7)

The "Golden Rule" tells us that we need to treat each other like we would like to be treated. Sometimes we need to know how our spouse wants to be treated, and act that way.

Be quick to forgive, quick to honor the other person. Always take your differences to God, the one who invented marriage in the first place. Always see yourselves as one. We all have different habits, IQ's, different educational levels and backgrounds. We all have different personalities.

Show appreciation for each other. There really is a way to solve problems without screaming at the top of your voice. We need to learn how to control our spirit. Praying together is important. "The family that prays together stays together."

Lord, when I am wrong, make me willing to change. When I am right, make me easy to live with. So strengthen me that the power of my example will exceed the authority of my rank.
Pauline H. Peters

Sometimes we have to forgive and forget the past. We have to "start over" to make things work. It's like the coach for our baseball team. He told the team that they were going to have to completely start over, because this was the worst team he had ever seen. "Sit down," he said as he held up a bat. "Now this is a baseball bat. This is a ball. When the pitcher throws the ball, the bat is supposed to hit the ball.: We started over.

Sometimes men cause the problems in the marriage. Other times women do. It's rarely big things that cause the worst problems, it's often seemingly insignificant things that happen over and over that eventually wear a sore spot.

The only way to get the best of an argument is to avoid it.
Dale Carnegie

Some wives bother men with backseat driving. She may nearly wear out the carpet on her side pushing on a brake that isn't there. Now they even make mats with a brake pedal for that kind of driver. Men frequently disturb their wives by ignoring them.

We need to take our differences, forget the little petty things and close the door to the problems in our lives. Fighting in the home will destroy us.

1) Humble yourself

2) Pray and seek God's face

3) Turn from our wicked ways

God will heal a marriage. (II Chronicles 7:14)

We must work to build or rebuild a marriage. Marriage is under attack. People who have been married more than forty years are getting divorces.

Proverbs 18:22 "Whoso findeth a wife findeth a good thing, and obtaineth favor of the Lord."

The next two pages are a marriage check list. Each of you take a few minutes to evaluate yourself, then your mate, and compare notes. Be honest, it's not a competition, more for information and to know what needs work.

HUSBAND'S CHECK LIST

RATE YOURSELF ON A SCALE OF 1 TO 10, WITH 10 BEING THE HIGHEST AND 1 BEING THE WORST.

_____.I married the right person.

_____.I have been as nice to her since our marriage as I was before.

_____.I am totally bonded to my wife and have eyes for no one else.

_____.I really see my wife and I as one.

_____.We have a Christian home.

_____.I always do my best to provide what my wife needs.

_____.I am a good sexual partner to her.

_____.I sacrifice my own interest to do what she wants.

_____.I tell her every day that I love and appreciate her.

_____.I do little things she likes to please her.

_____.I listen when she talks and show interest.

_____.We never go to sleep angry at each other.

_____.I don't talk about her faults to cover my own failures.

_____.We pray daily and read God's word together.

_____.I sometimes control my sexual needs in order to accommodate her.

_____.I am working on being a good husband and father.

_____.We attend church faithfully.

WIFE'S CHECK LIST

RATE YOURSELF ON A SCALE OF 1 TO 10, WITH 10 BEING THE HIGHEST AND 1 THE WORST.

_____.I married the right person.

_____.I have been as nice to him since our marriage as I was before.

_____.I am totally bonded to my husband and have eyes for no one else.

_____.I really see my husband and I as one.

_____.We have a Christian home.

_____.I always do my best to provide what my husband needs.

_____.I am a good sexual partner to him.

_____.I sacrifice my own interest to do what he wants.

_____.I tell him every day that I love and appreciate him.

_____.I do little things he likes to please him.

_____.I listen when he talks and show interest.

_____.We never go to sleep angry at each other.

_____.I don't talk about his faults to cover my own failures.

_____.We pray daily and read God's word together.

_____.I sometimes control my sexual needs in order to accommodate him.

_____.I am working on being a good wife and mother.

_____.We attend church faithfully.

NOTES

1. Commit yourself to having a great marriage.

2. Do II Chronicles 7:14

3. Make necessary changes.

TOP THREE CHANGES TO MAKE!

(Write after Marriage check list is done).

1.

2.

3.

12

DIVINE BLESSING VS LUCK

IN THIS CHAPTER:

CASEY STENGEL

JERRY SAVELLE

CHAPTER TWELVE

DIVINE BLESSING VS LUCK

Many of us, probably even most of us, have a few "pet superstitions." We don't do something a certain way because we were told as children that it was "unlucky." Or we may "knock on wood" after talking about some good thing that has happened. If someone asks us why, we probably laugh and deny that we really believe in the act, but that it "can't hurt." Luck, fate and the roll of the dice are the way some people live. They have never gotten beyond this.

I don't believe in luck, neither good nor bad. Things are not run by luck. I do believe in the divine blessing of God.

Suppose that a corporation was run by luck. If luck determines who does what and who goes where, every business in the world would fall apart. We can't assume that great businesses were organized on the basis of luck, that all the names were put in a hat and drawn to decide who had what position. It sounds stupid. Luck has nothing to do with it. Their success is organized and planned for.

People say "Man, it was lucky that I had that idea." Such things are not luck. Start trusting God for all His blessings.

We need to take a look at what appears to be someone's "good luck." You'll not find any luck. You'll find someone who prepared and planned and worked. They acquired the needed tools, education, knowledge, and from that their success "just happened." They learned how to manage right.

> **The secret of successful managing is to keep the five guys who hate you away from the four guys who haven't made up their minds yet.**
> **Casey Stengel**
> Major League Baseball Team Manager

Look at someone who has had "bad luck." They had a set back. Don't waste your time thinking that you can change "luck" in your life. There is no such thing. We don't become successful through "luck."

Success comes from doing what God wants us to do. We don't count on luck for victory in our life; nor for our marriage, for the car to run, or to be a winner.

I thought as a child that if someone was really rich and blessed, they were probably crooked. Or it was fate, it was luck. They were dishonest. Maybe the roll of the dice took them to their wealth. Don't believe it.

Some think like an old man, who lay in bed dying. He said to his wife, "When I limped home from the war, you were waiting for me. When I was released from Dachau at the end of the World War II, you were by my side."

Overcome with emotion he continued, "When we sold everything to start a business and it went broke and left us penniless, there you were. Now, as I breathe my last breath, here you stand by my bed side. Honey, I'm telling you, you're a jinx."

> When the storms of life strike, it's what
> happens *in* you that will determine
> what happens *to* you.
>
> Jerry Savelle

NOTES

1. Do not believe in luck, fate or roll of the dice in any manor.

2. Believe in Gods divine blessings for you.

TOP THREE CHANGES TO MAKE!

1.

2.

3.

13

THE JESUS FACTOR

IN THIS CHAPTER:

BILLY JOE DAUGHERTY

F. F. BOSWORTH

CHAPTER THIRTEEN
THE JESUS FACTOR

Sometimes we don't take into consideration the changes that will take place because of the *Jesus Factor.* Hebrews 7:25 "Wherefore He is able also to save them to the uttermost that come to God by Him, seeing He ever liveth to make intercession for them." Jesus is interceding for us, to be sure we have better treatment.

SIMON PETER

The *Jesus Factor* allowed Peter to walk on water during a severe storm. It also saved him when he got his eyes off of Jesus.

Luke 22:31 "The Lord said, 'Simon, Simon, behold, Satan hath desired to sift you as wheat: but I have prayed for you, that **thy faith fail not**." (Luke 22:31) This is the *Jesus Factor*.

A CITY

"He beheld the city, and wept over it." (Luke 19:41) Here was the *Jesus Factor* for a city.

A FAMILY

Jesus was concerned about the grief that a family felt. He wept because of the death of Lazarus. (John 11:33-36) His concern was obvious to those who were there.

DISCIPLES

John 17 records the concerned prayer of Jesus for his disciples. His prayer was extended down through the centuries even to us. The prayer didn't ask that we be taken out of the world, but that we be protected and kept from evil. This is the *Jesus Factor*. "At that day ye shall ask in my name, and I say not unto you, that I will pray the Father for you." (John 16:26)

A DAUGHTER

The examples of Jesus concern are many, the woman with the issue of blood, Jairus' daughter, the centurion's servant, the widow of Nain, blind people who were healed, the epileptic boy. The touch of Jesus has power to heal and meet needs.

MOTHER IN LAW

Peter's mother-in law was healed of a fever because Jesus was concerned. (Matthew 8:14,15)

A CROWD

Five thousand were gathered on the hillside of Galilee. Jesus was concerned because He knew that they must be hungry. The *Jesus Factor* multiplied the lunch of a child into more than enough to feed this multitude.

When the *Jesus Factor* takes over in your life, you can have more than enough. Jesus prayer in the Garden of Gethsemane asked that the will of the Father be done.

HEALING

The *Jesus Factor* cleansed leprosy, healed illness, raised the dead.

The *Jesus Factor* working through Peter raised Dorcas. It healed the lame man at the Gate Beautiful. Peter was released from prison.

SAUL

It also stopped Saul dead in his tracks and changed him from one of the worst persecutors of the Church into Paul, the apostle. It protected the crew of the ship on the Island of Melita, and caused an earthquake in Philippi which resulted in the conversion of the jailer.

God does not give victory over the world just to a select few. He gives an overcoming victory to every person that is born again.
Billy Joe Daugherty

Jesus is our example. "Christ also suffered for us: leaving His example, that ye should follow in His steps." (I Peter 2:21)

"Whoever claims to live in Him must walk as Jesus did." (I John 2:6 NIV) He is our example. Jesus told us that He had given us an example. (John 13:15)

The *Jesus Factor* will give us freedom. "Ye shall know the truth, and the truth shall set you free." He is a deliverer. He gives us power. (Luke 10:19) He promised that nothing would hurt us. Jesus is our freedom. He is our savior. He is our Lord.

OTHERS

The *Jesus Factor* is love, it is concern for others. It brings us forgiveness and inner peace. The *Jesus* Factor brings security. Jude 24 says that He is able to keep us, even through eternity.

When the *Jesus Factor* is working, we can do "all things through Christ." (Philippians 4:13) He'll supply all of our needs (v. 19). Whatever we need will be supplied because of the *Jesus Factor*.

**Faith does not wait for walls to fall down.
Faith shouts them down.**
F. F. Bosworth

The *Jesus Factor* will relieve discouragement. He tells us not to be discouraged. (John 14:1) He told us to give Him our worries and cares.

It will take care of loneliness, of uncertainty. God is our refuge.

You can tell when the *Jesus Factor* isn't working. Anger and resentment will surface.

The *Jesus Factor* will allow us to work miracles. Jesus himself said that we would do greater works than He had done, because He was going back to Heaven. (John 14:12)

The Lord will take care of us even in extreme difficulty because of the *Jesus Factor* (II Corinthians 4:8,9) He has promised to go with us in these times, not to keep us from having trouble.

The difference between winning and losing in each life is the *Jesus Factor*. It will bring out the best of who we are and what we can do. It will give us authority in our life.

NOTES

1. Believe the Jesus Factor can take over in your life.

2. Start thanking the Lord daily for working in your life.

TOP THREE CHANGES TO MAKE!

1.

2.

3.

14

CHANGING YOUR FUTURE

IN THIS CHAPTER:

CHAPTER FOURTEEN
CHANGING YOUR FUTURE

Jesus always had his thoughts on His Father and His Will. We can also have the mind of Christ. Philippians 2:5

To change our future, we must change our thinking. When a women marries a man, she usually thinks she can change this man. When a man marries a woman, he thinks that she will never change. Actually, both are wrong, we all change, sometimes for the better, sometimes for the worse. Their thinking needs to change. They need to rearrange their mental furniture.

HI-JACKED

Many almost happy marriages, successful futures, conceivably successful businesses and potentially large churches have been highjacked by thinking wrongly. Our thinking has to change, if we're going to change our future. A shift in how we look at things is a necessity. The world is constantly talking divorce, we should emphasize the strength of marriage. When businesses fall apart around you, believe that God will see you through. Believe that revival is coming to your church, and God will change an entire community. You can reach your goals when your thinking is changed. You need to rearrange your mental furniture. Romans 12:2 tells us to not be conformed to the things of this world, but to be transformed by the "renewing of our mind." I hear that the "renewing of your mind" is a New Age phrase. It's a Bible phrase. New Age is only appropriating it, they didn't invent it.

We can tackle any challenge. Miracles really happen when our thinking changes. Abraham changed his natural way of thinking, and began praying for a child. (Genesis 15:2-6) He and Sarah even took things into his own hands and fathered Ishmael, but God answered and Isaac was born. (Genesis 21:1-3)

Joshua was another one who changed his natural thinking and made history. (Joshua 10:12-14)

He commanded the sun and moon to stand still, and they did for the space of an entire day.

> **If you want to change your life,**
> **you have to change your confession.**
> **John Osteen**

King Darius changed his natural thinking. When he was forced by his own decree to cast Daniel into a den of lions, he declared to Daniel that "your God will deliver you." (Daniel 6)

Elijah caused a three and a half year drought. Then he called down fire from heaven. He changed the future. (I Kings 18:21-39)

Jesus came on the scene and changed the thinking and the future of the world. He performed miracles, healed the sick, fed multitudes, cleansed the leper and raised the dead. He changed the natural thinking of the people to believe that there are miracles available for them. And He said that we would do greater things than He did.

> If you can dream it, you can do it.
> ....This whole thing was started
> by a mouse.
>
> **Walt Disney**

LIMITS

We need to take the limits off of ourselves and God and change our thinking. We can tackle any challenge. Paul told us to think on things that are true and honest and just and pure and lovely and good. Paul faced many crises, yet he could say that God's peace kept his heart and mind. He learned how to change his future.

I tell this story often. I was working late at my office when a good friend, Woody Clark, of Woodpecker Trucks called and asked me what I was doing. I replied that I was trying to work something out. He quickly retorted, "Well, have you ever thought of having God work it out?"

I started to interrupt with, "Yes, but...."

"God can take care of it, Ken," he insisted.

I tried again, "I tried that, but....."

"God will handle it," was his response.

The next time I got a little farther. "Woody, you know I trust God, but...."

He interrupted me again. Woody said, "Ken, go home, go to bed, rest in peace. Just shut up and prove that you trust God. Don't make the need bigger than God is."

I listened to Woody. I went home and got a good night's rest. God worked the problem out.

Some people change jobs, friends, cars, homes, even mates; but they never think of changing themselves.
Jack Holt

Paul stated that "all things work together for good." He did not say that all things were good, but if we trust God, he will make things work out and change our future for His glory.

We need to "renew our mind" so we can receive what God has for us.

Consider how hard it is to change yourself and you'll understand what little chance you have of changing others.
Jacob M. Braude

We've got to start resisting and rebuking the devil in our lives. We must have victory in our lives.

If you're a Christian, it is time you start binding Satan and loose his hold on your life. You can bind Satan for years but you need to start loosing his hold on you rebuking and resisting him.

Have faith and rearrange your mental furniture so your thoughts are filled with God's ways.

Faith and works should travel side by side, step after step, like the legs of men walking. First faith, then works, then faith again, then works again until you can hardly distinguish which is the one and which is the other.

William Booth

Pray this prayer:

IN JESUS NAME..... I come against you, Satan, binding you and your past hold on my life. I block you, Satan from any future hold or effect on me, from this day forth. MY life is now in God's hand, and I want to have the mind of Christ, His thoughts, His way, His purposes. I rebuke and resist you, Satan and take back all you have stolen from me.

Jesus, I ask forgiveness for wrong, negative thinking. Create in me a clear heart and mind, helping me to serve you with all my heart, obeying all your commandments. Help to keep my thoughts pleasing you. Thank you for hearing and answering me.

Amen

NOTES

1. Take limits off of yourself.

2. Bind and loose Satan from your life and future.

TOP THREE CHANGES TO MAKE

1.

2.

3.

FINAL NOTES

TO HELP YOU REARRANGE YOUR MENTAL FURNITURE

Final Notes

Here are some things that have helped me. I trust they will bless your life with positive results and help you rearrange your mental furniture.

1. Begin every day with God as your partner.

2. Rebuke, resist and reject anything that Satan puts in your way.

3. Believe that God is bigger than Satan in your life.

4. Be a forgiving person.

5. Believe that God intends for you to solve problems, not make them.

6. Never panic when a challenge comes your way.

7. Stay cheerful, even when you're not happy. If you have a flat tire, you're not happy, but you can still be cheerful.

8. Control circumstances, don't let them control you.

9. Interrupt negative thoughts that come to your thought life.

10. Believe that God will see you through any situation, and that everything will be all right.

11. Believe that God will return many times over that which Satan has taken from you.

12. Attend church faithfully and win others to Christ.

13. Be a tither and a giver.

14. Fast and pray. (Matthew 17:14)

15. Obey the commandments of God.

16. Be a reader of God's Word. It is food for our spiritual lives. A snack on Sunday morning is not enough to feed you for the whole week.

17. Let your faith grow. II Thessalonians 1:3 talks about our faith growing.

18. Believe God to think bigger.

19. Get involved in your church.

20. Start praising God daily in advance for miracles.

I do these three things daily:

1. I ask God to be with me.

2. I believe that He will answer my prayers.

3. I thank him in advance for all that He has done for me and what He is going to continue to do.

OTHER PRODUCTIONS
BY
KEN GAUB

AVAILABLE THROUGH YOUR CHRISTIAN BOOKSTORE OR CALL KEN GAUB WORLD WIDE MINISTRIES 1-509-575-1965

BOOKS:
GOD'S GOT YOUR NUMBER
ANSWERS TO QUESTIONS YOU ALWAYS
      WANTED TO KNOW
DREAMS, PLANS, GOALS
SKY HIGH FAITH

VIDEOS:
SMOKIN' SMOKE (comedy)
BALANCED LIFE SEMINAR (5 tape series)

Answers to
Questions You've
Always Wanted to
Ask

Dreams, Plans,
Goals

God's Got Your
Number

Sky High Faith